MENSWEAR TRENDS

Bloomsbury Visual Arts

An imprint of Bloomsbury Publishing Plc

50 Bedford Square	1385 Broadway
London	New York
WC1B 3DP	NY 10018
UK	USA

www.bloomsbury.com

BLOOMSBURY and the Diana logo are trademarks of Bloomsbury Publishing Plc

© Bloomsbury Publishing Plc, 2018

Aki Choklat has asserted his right under the Copyright, Designs and Patents Act, 1988, to be identified as Author of this work.

British Library Cataloguing-in-Publication Data
A catalogue record for this book is available from the British Library.

ISBN:
PB: 978-1-4725-9171-5
ePDF: 978-1-4725-9172-2

Library of Congress Cataloging-in-Pulication Data
Names: Choklat, Aki, author.
Title: Menswear trends / Aki Choklat.
Description: New York : Bloomsbury Visual Arts, 2017. | Series: Required Reading Range | Includes bibliographical references and index.
Identifiers: LCCN 2015044111| ISBN 9781472591715 (pbk. : alk. paper) | ISBN 9781472591722 (epdf : alk. paper)
Subjects: LCSH: Men's clothing. | Fashion—Forecasting.
Classification: LCC TT617 .C48 2016 | DDC 646.4/02—dc23 LC record available at http://lccn.loc.gov/2015044111

Cover design: Louise Dugdale
Cover image © Ruggero Mengoni
Cover model: Stefan Fugger

Typeset by hoopdesign.co.uk
Printed and bound in China

To find out more about our authors and books visit www.bloomsbury.com. Here you will find extracts, author interviews, details of forthcoming events and the option to sign up for our newsletters.

MENSWEAR TRENDS

Aki Choklat

Bloomsbury Visual Arts
An imprint of Bloomsbury Publishing Plc

BLOOMSBURY
LONDON · OXFORD · NEW YORK · NEW DELHI · SYDNEY

CONTENTS

INTRODUCTION

Interest in menswear has seen an exponential growth in recent years, which is why many companies have started to cater to the menswear market. This textbook is an introduction to the fastest growing sector in fashion: the as-yet-untapped world of menswear trends. It will help you to better understand the future male consumer while anticipating the needs and desires of this customer. Many fashion design schools focus on creativity in teaching, often forgetting the realities of the post-graduate world. In *Menswear Trends,* the gap between creativity and commercial needs will be filled.

Many magazines are devoted to menswear, such as *Fantastic Man* and *Hero* in Europe and *Popeye*, *Free&Easy* and *Huge* from Japan. Coverage of international menswear fashion weeks has now crossed over to mainstream media in newspapers and on television. Social media also reveals that men have also become more trend-conscious.

This book analyses trends in menswear and explores factors that make menswear the most interesting, dynamic and fast-moving sector of fashion at the moment. Menswear revenue, according to many reports, will surpass that of womenswear soon (Euromonitor Research 2015, Geoghegan 2017, 'Growth' 2016). Men are more interested in their appearance and are spending more on apparel and accessories such as shoes, bags and watches. Trends and the fashion forecasting

business has been reported to be a multibillion dollar (USD) growing industry, yet there are only a few globally recognized agencies that work with fashion and consumer trends. Trend forecasting companies have now started to realize the impact of the expanding menswear sector.

This book examines the connection between menswear and culture, as well as socioeconomic factors that enable us to foresee the direction of fashion. It will analyse not just culture and behaviour, but also how they evolve and influence what men wear. *Menswear Trends* will explain how to anticipate trends using research and specific methodologies. With this book you will be studying the origins of trends, how these ideas filter into the fashion cycle, what individuals *can* do with this information, and what companies *currently* do with the information. You will also explore suggestions on how companies, media and individuals could most benefit. This book will be valuable not only to students but also to anyone interested in fashion and menswear.

Menswear Trends starts by looking at some key sociohistorical events. These events influenced what people wore, outlining an interesting past for basic menswear items. It is essential to understand how past events have influenced the menswear customer of yesterday in order to predict which key events of today will affect and inspire menswear in the future – and how.

We move on to the history of trends analysis as corporate services, tracing it to the beginning of the twentieth century, when there was a growing need to produce apparel that people wanted; therefore, accurate foresight was needed. The knowledge of trend history and how it relates to the needs of the industry is directly relevant to the existence of agencies today. We will introduce some of the most important contemporary agencies through the 'Industry Insight' feature in each chapter, giving you a unique and valuable opportunity to better understand how they operate. Most fashion companies use agency services, which is why fundamental trend agency knowledge is essential.

The central theme of the book is how and where to gather trend material; what to do with this information; and how trends can be translated to the end user, individual or company. Some of the key questions this book addresses are:

- What are the new menswear norms?
- How do we stay competitive and ahead of the game?
- Who is the male customer of tomorrow?
- How can we provide product that men will need and desire in the future?
- What can a brand do to be on trend (instead of copying other brands and catwalks)?

0.1

Menswear Trends will enable you to become both forecasters and trend thinkers – and to bring new ideas, innovation and strategies to men's fashion.

0.1
Menswear trends come and go; they fade away only to return in a new, slightly altered state. Some trends take decades to reappear, whereas others return in a few seasons.

1.1

1.1
*The Nonchalant
Dandy*, 1901, by
Edward Loevy.
The painting
depicts how in the
early twentieth
century even
leisurely activities
involved rather
formal dress.

1

Society, Menswear and Trends

LEARNING OBJECTIVES

- Explore the key moments in history that shaped what men wore in order to understand the relationship between past and present menswear.
- Analyse historical factors and their role in dress.
- Learn how trend agencies were born out of a specific need in the clothing marketplace.
- Examine the connection between society and menswear.
- Discuss the role and the influence of youth subcultures in menswear.

INTRODUCTION

Fashion and menswear are often influenced by socioeconomic and cultural influences in society, and this has been the case since their earliest days. A historical foundation of trend knowledge is necessary for better analysis and foresight; we can learn much from historical patterns about what men will want to buy in seasons to come. In this chapter we discuss the importance of history and its role in menswear trend practice by looking at some key events and how they influenced what men have worn. Historical information is essential to understand how ideas and men's dress concepts came to be; having this basic awareness will provide a strong framework for analyzing the current norms and directions of men's fashion.

In this chapter we also examine menswear concepts and terminology, which are essential tools for writing and speaking about products to a client or to a wider audience. The basic menswear terms and concepts may be familiar to fashion students, but they may be new to marketing and brand students, who will need to know these fundamentals when working with menswear.

It is also important to be well versed in trend concepts, their historical progression and why there was and is a need for trend services. Understanding the historical path helps to clarify where we are now with trends, and defining the key terms will provide a strong starting point for menswear trends in particular.

1.2
A group of fashionable men from *Le Follet*, a Parisian fashion plate magazine from 1839. Note the man in the middle wearing a dressing gown based on the Indian banyan, a favourite of the nineteenth-century creative set.

1.2

1.3

1.3
Today's menswear
often references the
past. In this Gucci
SS 2016 catwalk,
clear references
are made to
bohemian looks.
An absinthe green
dressing gown;
in its previous
incarnation, it was
popular with the
creative set of the
nineteenth century.

1.4
Popular culture
has always been an
important driver for
trends to spread.
Here, Malcolm
McLaren, owner
of the boutique
SEX and manager
of the Sex Pistols,
is photographed
in 1976 London,
shortly before
punk subculture
became recognized
worldwide.

TRENDS DEFINED

Merriam-Webster (2017) defines a 'trend' as something that follows 'a general course', showing a 'tendency' or a 'shift'. Trends by definition can be anything that gains momentum and moves in a direction. 'Trending' has become a buzzword in social media and online portals, used to catch people's attention and to steer traffic to various different areas.

In contemporary society trends are often associated with design and the fashion world. A trend in the fashion world is generally a style of dress or other behaviour that is slowly gaining momentum and popularity. All aspects of fashion, such as colour, silhouette and accessories, can be separately analysed as trends.

In contemporary fashion some of the most important influencers are the designers themselves. Perhaps the most important menswear influencer of the past twenty years is Hedi Slimane, who introduced the slim suit for men in the early 2000s. This new cut was imitated and adopted by many, influencing the men's silhouette for well over a decade. Another big influencer in menswear is Rick Owens, who introduced more unisex, androgynous looks for menswear. Longer silhouette, hip-hugging T-shirts layered with tank tops have gone mainstream recently. And today Raf Simons continues with his eponymous collections, merging art with fashion.

Trends are not only limited to tangible things such as clothing; they include changing attitudes and general behaviour. Societal factors such as music, food culture and sports can trigger menswear trends. Societal trends often anticipate fashion trends, and it is important to understand both because they are closely intertwined.

MENSWEAR DEFINED

Menswear is simply something designed to be worn on the male body – whether apparel, footwear or accessories. Apparel can be divided into several subcategories, such as casual wear, formal wear, outerwear and sportswear (to name a few). It is important to note that the above definition of menswear is in the most general terms. There is an ever-changing vocabulary that continues to further define menswear.

One of the main changes in the twentieth century that has also influenced these categories is the 'casualization' of dress in menswear. Ever since leisure activities, including travel and sports, started to be part of our lifestyle, we have looked for more comfort and ease in clothing. The beauty of trends and rapidly evolving fashion is that rules are constantly broken, re-written or re-defined in order to bring new elements to men's fashion language.

MENSWEAR AND ITS RELATIONSHIP TO THE CHANGING MOODS OF SOCIETY

Trends can be introduced to society through many channels. One of the bigger influencers is societal change, which shapes the opinion and attitudes of people that will ultimately influence what we wear. Historical influences, political figures, pop idols and designers are also drivers of menswear trends.

1.4

MENSWEAR AND SOCIETY

Let's look at some major historical moments to understand how changes in society can influence menswear. One of the most significant historical influences relating to dress was the court of Louis XIV, the Sun King (1638–1715), a true trendsetter of his time. His court's lavish dress styles were an inspiration to many. Perhaps one of the most visible items that spread to other countries was the Talon Rouge, a red-heeled shoe that became the style of choice for many European courts. The French ruler required all the members of the court to wear shoes with red heels as a symbol of elite nobility. The lower classes of society were not permitted to wear them.

This type of restrictive decree or regulation – called sumptuary law – existed not only in Europe but also across other cultures. Sumptuary laws were designed to halt spending by the aspirational middle class and to reinforce class differences so that the nobility could maintain its superiority through the use of clear status symbols. Today clothing is regulated under rare circumstances, such as when it might relate to military gear or religious laws. However, although sumptuary laws are usually not formally stated, they are still very much part of the unspoken 'rule book' of fashion – particularly of menswear.

CONTINENTAL INFLUENCES

The expansion of travel options during the late 1700s brought continental influences to menswear in the UK and the capitals of Europe in the form of Dandyism. In fact, The Dandies were one of the most influential groups that shaped and created a foundation for modern menswear. Beau Brummel (born George Bryan Brummell, 1778–1840) was at the forefront of this cult of fashion, introducing various new ways of dressing. It was to his great advantage that the Prince Regent (later King George the IV of the United Kingdom) was a friend and adopter of the Dandy way of dressing. Brummel had rituals that sound extreme, even by today's standard of cleanliness: soaking in hot baths for hours and refusing to wear perfume simply because he needed none. Daily bathing rituals in Europe were not practiced until over a hundred years later.

The Dandy's fitted sleek new silhouette brought about the development of the contemporary suit. The modern trouser, a Dandy heritage, was developed from 'pantaloons', a type of trouser preferred by these fashionable men. Even the British Navy was inspired by the Dandy bee-line waist, and adopted the fashion to naval dress. This caused some questioning of the masculinity of the Navy, and ultimately the whole empire (Miller 2007). Dandyism is often associated with outlandish dressing and colourful ornamentation; however, the original

1.5

Brummelian Dandyism was more about understated dress, favouring simple, muted colours. 'To be well dressed, you must not be noticed' (d'Aurevilly 1897: 68).

The influence of Dandyism did not only pertain to clothes; it related to attitude and other facets of existence. Dandyism became a way of life.

1.5
A famous portrait of the Sun King, Louis XIV, by Hyacinthe Rigaud shows the lavish lifestyles of the noble class. Exposing calf muscles was important stylistically at the time, as were the red heels that only the noble class were allowed to wear.

1.6

1.7

1.6
Beau Brummel became one of the most influential figures in early menswear history by introducing men to the cult of dressing.

1.7
In a fashion plate by French artist Francois Courboin entitled 'The Great Longchamps Day', France, 1820, men appear in strapped trousers, top hats, cravats and boots with elongated toes and delicate bow slippers.

1.8
Advertisement for men's suits by Sears, Roebuck & Company, 1897.

MENSWEAR AS COMMODITY IN POST-INDUSTRIAL REVOLUTION

The nineteenth century was an era that helped shape menswear history and created the foundations for contemporary menswear. Dandyism was a great influence initially, giving men new opportunities to express style, but what really fuelled the fires of menswear was the industrial revolution and all it brought.

When machinery was developed for the garment industry, it became possible to produce clothing in larger quantities than ever before. After the end of the industrial revolution (1830–1840), thirty-six different companies produced sewing machines in the United States alone. Sales increased from around 2,500 machines in 1853 to around 50,000 in 1863 and to more than 667,500 in 1873 (Eves et al. 2017). This rapid development occurred not only in sewing, but also in textile and yarn/thread production. Affordable clothing became more widely available, and this affected socioeconomic relationships between people.

This era also saw a rise in men's love of sport. Sportswear aided the decline of elitist codes because most men wore similar outfits, regardless of their rank in society. Young men wore their sports clothing outside the athletic arena, paving the way for this huge sector of fashion to expand.

After the industrial revolution, towards the end of the nineteenth century, fashion and menswear started to take a more commercial form. Style was no longer just for the select few; fashion had become something that many could purchase and enjoy.

1.9
Fashion and
menswear
had become a
commodity that
more and more
men could enjoy,
as seen in this late-
nineteenth-century
photograph.
Advances in
photography
helped fashion to
be marketed more
effectively.

1.9

FASHION AS COMMODITY

Due to exponential growth in manufacturing, there was a new need for marketing and fashion strategy. Better and cheaper printing allowed catalogue shopping to evolve, and wider distribution became possible as more efficient postal and road systems developed. The fashion industry established itself and started to provide something that was not available before: variety.

The main fashion houses started to develop during the early part of the twentieth century. Major department stores (including Sears, Roebuck & Company, Montgomery Ward and Macy's in the United States and Marks and Spencer in the United Kingdom) began to offer more options for men.

Variety and the Need for Trend Direction

Growing production resulted in a need to source more raw materials and to consider options such as dyes and material colours. In 1915 the Textile Color Card Association of the U.S., Inc. (now known as The Color Association of the United States (CAUS)) started to sell colour advice to the hat, glove and hosiery manufacturers, becoming the trendsetting industry of its time. This early trend work based colour suggestions on the seasons and demand, offering predictions about what would sell. CAUS was founded on the needs of the textile and fashion industries but currently provides information for a variety of different industries.

1.10

1.10
Advertising and variety, as seen in this catalogue page of male winter fashions from Bruner Woolens from the 1920s, provided men with new dressing opportunities. The increasing variety in goods drove manufacturers' need for advice about what to produce next.

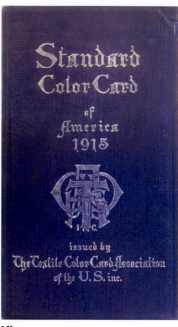

1.11

Retail and the Common Male Consumer

Many companies had already started selling menswear in department stores in the late 1800s, but in the 1920s the United Kingdom's Marks and Spencer saw the opportunity to sell affordable clothing, such as dungarees and coats, to the working class man. The birth of visual merchandising and other entrepreneurial skills was instrumental in the development of the menswear industry.

By the Second World War, men's role in society was focused on the war effort, and this had a direct influence on menswear. Fabrics were scarce and often rationed, which influenced the width of trousers and jacket structure. The relationship between men and uniforms greatly influenced casual wear. Many aspects of the military uniforms of this era, such as camouflage, khakis and combat boots, have become menswear seasonal classics.

During the 1940s producers of goods became increasingly aware that they needed to know what people wanted in order to provide it. One of the most interesting early attempts to understand the consumer is Faber Birren's 1945 *Selling with Color*. Birren's analysis pre-dates all our contemporary customer behaviour and trend theories. The book focuses on colour, which is still considered to be the deciding factor in apparel choices, but it has many sections on trends (the word is mentioned close to thirty times): 'While trends are difficult to define and no less difficult to anticipate, a certain amount of reasonable order will be found in them' (57). Birren also discusses how economic and social conditions affect trends; for example, the end of the Great Depression brought bright colours to cars, interiors and kitchens, where they had never been seen before.

1.11
It could be argued that the trend forecasting industry started when the Textile Color Card Association of the U.S., Inc., offered the first colour suggestions for the apparel industry in 1915.

1.12
1930 Spring colour card forecast for the woolen industry. The idea of forecasting was already widely accepted by the woolen manufacturers of the time.

1.12

THE ORIGINS OF TREND FORECASTING

The word 'trend' was first used in 1863 in a sense of 'have a general tendency' ('trend' 2010). However, it was not used as an indicator of style until a few decades later, when fashion and menswear became a more widely accepted commodity.

During the early twentieth century, the wheels of production had started to turn, and the hunger for more product started to affect everything, including branding, marketing and visual merchandising. Product becoming available in numerous variations was perhaps the most significant cause of the birth of trends and trend forecasting. Manufacturers, retailers and shoppers needed direction in this new world of fashion commerce.

Youth and Early Trend Reporting

Early trend services targeted both the manufacturer and the retail consumer just as they do today. The Color Association of the United States (CAUS) is one example of a consultancy advising a manufacturer about what to make. Periodicals, on the other hand, influenced the retail consumer. The first recorded fashion magazine, mainly geared to men, was the French periodical *Mercure Galant*, which was issued between 1678 and 1714. The issues often had seasonal suggestions on what to wear mixed in with society gossip, poetry and art. It was a prototype for contemporary fashion magazines.

Several trade magazines, such as the New York–based *The Clothier and Furnisher*, used predictive language to help manufacturers navigate the already complex clothing trade. In their 1894 issue the necktie was a topic of conversation: 'There is in the greater trend towards the "safer" design in all phases of men's furnishing, and incitement to greater freedom of purchase' ('Furnishing Editorial' 1894: 75). However, the magazine that really set the blueprint for today's menswear magazines was *Fashion*, published in London between 1898 and 1905 (Shannon 2006). The magazine offered suggestions as well as predictive points of view to influence the consumer. To have a dedicated menswear magazine in the 1890s was simply revolutionary.

1.13

1.13
American Varsity
styles targeted
trend-conscious
young men in this
1917 advert.

Men were assumed not to pay great attention to their appearances during that era.

In early trend history, *Fashion* was important because it set out to advise the reader on what one ought to wear, paving the way for future trend influence in publications. Trend language and predictive ideology was implemented, making *Fashion* the first menswear publication with clear trend content geared towards the non-trade consumer.

However, one person saw a business opportunity in predictions for both manufacturers and retailers. Her name was Miss Tobé (neé Taubé Coller), and she provided Paris-based information to North American retailers and manufacturers. Miss Tobé might have been the first trend forecaster. As described in the *Delineator* magazine's April 1937 issue, 'Tobé isn't an oracle, she isn't a designer – she simply knows from experience, better than anyone else, what styles

you are going to like best and what will be most useful to you. From the great fashion salons of Paris, from tailored England, from America, she culls the newest and best of the season's creations. She goes to ultra-smart resorts; she keeps a weather eye on the world's best-dressed' (1937: 24). The TOBE Report, as it is known today, was later acquired by the Doneger Group (which has also been providing trend intelligence since 1946).

The early 1900s also birthed the Ivy League look (later known as 'Preppie' style). It was the most important menswear trend among American private college men that was actively reported to US menswear buyers. The Ivy League look was heavily influenced by sportswear, reaching its heyday in the mid-1900s. Clothes worn for sports were adopted for casual wear. The look included tweeds from golfing and V-neck sweaters from tennis. The Ivy League look later evolved to include the blazer, khakis and madras.

Apparel Arts, a menswear retail buying guide, first published in 1931, featured styling suggestions that understood the trend-hungry college students and their buying power. The magazine often reported campus fashions, including 'bankable' looks that retailers could count on selling well. They used their 'Fashion Forecast' page to predict the latest must-have key items for men. *Apparel Arts* was also one of the earlier magazines to use trend vocabulary, including

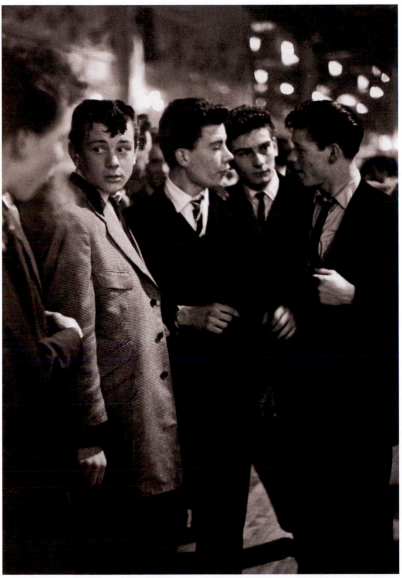

1.14

the words 'forecasting', 'fad' and the word 'trend' itself. A report from the Princeton campus in the summer of 1933 includes, 'Any question as to the national popularity of gabardine can be conclusively quashed – its tremendous acceptance at Princeton makes its subsequent mass popularity all over the country a bankable certainty' and, on plaid jackets, 'Glen Urquhart plaids are still extremely popular, but are most often noted in a new type which is a somewhat subdued Glen . . . In odd jackets, however, the opposite trend is noted – The Glen becoming bolder and more pronounced' ('Maytime' 1933).

1.14
Many subcultural movements, from Teddy Boys (as seen here in 1954) to Punks, later became trends as their elements filtered into mainstream fashions.

1.15

The magazine featured lavish colour illustrations and street styling, with photographs of men from the streets of New York, Palm Beach and London, before the contemporary 'street-style' concept even existed. *Apparel Arts* was a visionary publication, paving the way for all contemporary menswear magazines. Trends started to be used as a sales tool for US menswear buyers thanks largely to the Ivy League and the collegiate world.

Subcultural phenomena are often associated with youth; many of the major movements, such as Teddy Boys, Mods, Hippies and Punk, started as the rebellious dress codes of the young. These trends often spread around the world with the help of music, which is an effective medium for influencing people's decisions.

1.16

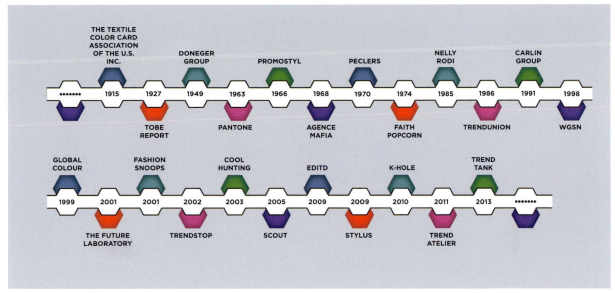

THE TEXTILE
COLOR CARD
ASSOCIATION
OF THE U.S.
INC.

DONEGER
GROUP

PROMOSTYL

PECLERS

NELLY
RODI

CARLIN
GROUP

1915 1927 1949 1963 1966 1968 1970 1974 1985 1986 1991 1998

TOBE
REPORT

PANTONE

AGENCE
MAFIA

FAITH
POPCORN

TRENDUNION

WGSN

GLOBAL
COLOUR

FASHION
SNOOPS

COOL
HUNTING

EDITD

K-HOLE

TREND
TANK

1999 2001 2001 2002 2003 2005 2009 2009 2010 2011 2013

THE FUTURE
LABORATORY

TRENDSTOP

SCOUT

STYLUS

TREND
ATELIER

1.17

MENSWEAR TRENDS TODAY

Menswear trends are described and analysed everywhere today – from magazines to social media. Although digital media has exploded in recent years, printed magazines are still an important part of menswear communication. Most menswear magazines have dedicated trends sections, with must-have items from the catwalk and retail stores. Similarly, newspapers report on fashion weeks and carry out their own analyses at the start of each season. This type of trend editorial is more an analysis of what is currently in the marketplace than a trend prediction. When trends appear in popular media, the term usually describes what is on offer at that time or what will appear next season. This type of reporting is analytical by nature rather than predictive.

Serious trend predictions and suggestions for the future usually appear in dedicated trend magazines, such as *Textile View* (http://view-publications .com). Trade shows often have dedicated trends presentations for menswear, whether they are raw material fairs or finished product events. Predictive trend practice is usually done by professional groups, such as WGSN and Trendstop.

1.15
Fashion designers are inspired by the past; subcultural elements give new life to old trends season after season. Here, Saint Laurent's AW 2014 reveals a 1950s Teddy Boy influence.

1.16
Menswear insights from Trendstop take trend direction cues from street and contemporary culture, including art.

1.17
Trends have become part of our common fashion vocabulary in the past twenty years, but many of the terms appeared over a hundred years ago. Here are a selection of some of the key agencies and services.

1.18

VOLKER KETTENISS
Head of Menswear, WGSN

Volker Ketteniss is Head of Menswear at WGSN, the world's leading trend forecasting agency. WGSN was established in 1998, pioneering the digital trend service platform.

How did you end up working with trends? After graduating from RCA in 1999, I worked as a menswear designer for smaller as well as large international brands. In 2008 the opportunity at WGSN came up, as head of the menswear team. Creative concept and collection development had always been a part of my job that I really enjoyed, and I was open to using my experience and skills in different ways. If you are looking to broaden your horizons, and are OK with not having physical garments at the end of the process, then trend forecasting offers an attractive mix. It has a wide cultural perspective and encourages a diverse range of talents – research, analysis, writing, photography, editing, curating and visual storytelling – but always returns to questions of design and commercial product development. So all your industry experience still counts, and editors at WGSN typically come from a variety of backgrounds: designers, buyers, merchandisers, as well as journalists. This kind of environment suited me quite well, and still does.

1.18
Volker Ketteniss is head of menswear at WGSN.

1.19
WGSN gathers intelligence from streets and catwalks to summarize the key trends, as seen in this example.

ARTISAN A/W 16/17   COLLECTION PLAN

1.19

1.20

When/how do you start working with the new season trends? Our main forecasts are published about eighteen months ahead of the actual season, but the internal process starts a few months prior to that. We have the luxury of access to a large number of specialists across all the relevant areas of the fashion market, but we are also looking at art and culture, film, music, consumer behaviour, technology and social media. At the beginning of each season, our global content teams get together in London and share their ideas of where trends are going in their respective areas and regions. From this we develop four big ideas, our Macro Trends, which serve as a framework of inspiration for the season ahead, alongside our colour, textile and materials forecasts. The Macro Trends are then applied back into the different categories – womenswear, menswear, youth, kids, active sport, denim, footwear and accessories – where they are distilled into tangible and relevant product ideas. Of course, this process does not remain in a bubble, but throughout the season gets constantly updated with trends emerging from catwalks, trade shows, retail and street style.

How has the world of trends and trend forecasting changed in the past years – specifically, menswear trend forecasting? Trend forecasting is information, and, like all information services, the industry has been completely transformed with the development of the Internet. WGSN pioneered the idea when it started in 1998, but in recent years most of the trend-relevant information has become available online, often for free: catwalk shows, look books, magazine editorials, e-commerce, street style and specialized blogs. However, the undigested volume of information quickly becomes unmanageable, making it hard for companies to stay on top of what's going on in an increasingly global marketplace, as it can require whole trend departments to sift through the information and separate what's relevant from what isn't.

The menswear market in particular has changed substantially over recent years and managed to step out from the shadow of women's fashion. With strong market growth rates, prominent events like Pitti Uomo and the independence of London Collections, menswear is getting a lot more attention. There is also a lively culture that has developed online, with blogs, magazines, street style, Tumblr and Pinterest inspiration feeds and well-curated online shopping.

1.20
An important part of WGSN trend direction is the collection plan that inspires designers to create on-trend collections.

REMASTER A/W 16/17   COLLECTION PLAN

1.21

What is the role of street style? Street style photography has played a big role in popularizing more sophisticated ideas about men's style and has made it both visible and accessible to the male consumer. It has helped to crystallize certain looks, like classic Italian tailoring à la Pitti Uomo, heritage denim and biker workwear, or high-fashion urban streetwear, alongside strong masculine attributes like big beards and tattoos.

As in womenswear, there is a risk of overexposure and commercial hi-jacking blurring the boundaries between real street style and brand advertising, but it feels less pronounced in menswear, and good quality street style photography will remain a strong influence.

Do you have a system or methodology you use for forecasting? I don't think you can devise a formula for it, more just a structure for the process. It's a combination of thorough analysis, experience and good instincts. Nowadays, data-based research is becoming increasingly important to supplement traditional trend forecasting. We have another product called WGSN INstock that can provide data and analysis gathered from online shopping websites. A lot of companies are interested in this kind of thing.

The further you try to project into the future, the harder it gets. Then it is helpful if you can think like a designer, and are able to find sources of inspiration and newness that are likely to resonate with other creatives in the industry.

1.21
Trend directions can vary from formal to casual, as seen here for the A/W 16/17 trend titled 'Remaster'.

What trade shows are important to visit (raw materials and finished product)?
Première Vision and Milano Unica still give the widest overview of what is going on; also good is the PV denim edition. For finished product Pitti Uomo is still the main contender to see every season, not just because of the great mix of brands but also the whole experience and the events around it. The combination of Capsule, MAN and Tranoï is worth seeing during Paris Fashion Week; Jacket Required in London and Seek in Berlin are also good.

What is the biggest difference between menswear and womenswear forecasting? The menswear market isn't driven as much by fast-changing trends as womenswear is. It operates within a smaller spectrum of established looks and items, and evolves at a slower pace. Most guys stick to a certain look that works for them within their peer group, and there is a fine line beyond which men's fashion can look weird. It's important to recognize that, and to be able to distinguish the finer details of trends that manage to stretch the boundaries enough to feel interesting and fresh, without pushing too far.

What cultural shift in the past years, in your opinion, has changed menswear?
There have been multiple factors involved. It probably really started in the wake of the recession, with men sharpening up their image to compete in a tightening job market, and many big brands refocusing on their roots and the kind of timeless product they were traditionally really good at, like classic tailoring, heritage denim and workwear. Money was still being spent, but it had to be on the right things.

The renewed interest in male fashion and grooming has been supported by a larger cultural trend towards a more masculine aesthetic, which has spread with the help of the Internet and created a more educated and demanding male consumer. Films and TV series such as *The Great Gatsby*, *Mad Men*, *Boardwalk Empire* and *Sons of Anarchy* have been a strong influence on fashion and grooming, but you can also see wider effects in design and technology. Car designs, for example, now look much sportier and aggressive than maybe ten years ago, which is likely related to cinema's ongoing fascination with sci-fi and superhero movies, all very male genres.

At the same time, new high-end developments in textile technology have helped elevate prominent sports and streetwear influences to catwalk designer level. So, while today's new menswear looks are still about ideas of smartness and considered styling, they feel more contemporary than vintage, even when referencing past decades.

How do you see the future of menswear? There is a lot happening in menswear now, and people are beginning to pay attention. The market has a growing momentum that suggests that a lot more is possible. There are more restrictions than in womenswear, but rules are traditionally more conducive to good design solutions than an anything-goes environment. So I am quite excited about the future of menswear.

1.22

BARBARA VINKEN
Professor and Author

Barbara Vinken (http://www.barbaravinken.de) is a scholar and Chair of Comparative and French Literature at the University of Munich. She is also the author of *Fashion Zeitgeist* – an essential trend read – in which she discusses the cyclical nature of fashion. In the book she questions 'originality', demonstrating the role of politics, philosophy and the past to influence a trend.

What were the main societal changes that influenced menswear in the 1700/1800s? Obviously, the French Revolution, which was even named as a fashion event: the 'sans culottes' came into power. 'Les pantalons' were the latest rage. The ideal of the bourgeois replaced the aristocrat as role model. Ostentatious beauty of the male was a no-go in modern times.

What were the societal factors that helped the birth of the Dandy? The disempowerment of the aristocracy, the rise of the bourgeois and its new ideology of the great renunciation of erotic masculinity. Whereas a Dandy is a 'clothes-wearing man', a man whose only profession and absolute occupation it is to wear clothes, the bourgeois has had to show in his clothes that he has more important things to take care of than the clothes he wears.

What was the role of Dandyism in menswear history? The Dandy was the motor of fashion.

Did Dandyism influence womenswear? Immensely. It is the single most dominating influence on the change in womenswear. Think of Coco Chanel, who said of herself that all she did was to translate menswear into womenswear. She did, of course, not mean just any man, but the dandy . . . his nonchalance, desinvolture, his refinement.

1.22
Barbara Vinken, a scholar and author of *Fashion Zeitgeist*.

1.23
Fashion Zeitgeist, Trends and Cycles in the Fashion System, by Barbara Vinken, is a key academic book in trends and fashion.

1.23

Was there a relationship between the development of military uniforms and Dandyism? Yes. The uniform was a relic from aristocratic times. It allowed – colourful, adorned, awfully well cut – the show-off of a beautiful, adorned male body. It proved to be absolutely dysfunctional, and during the First World War, even fatally dangerous. All of this glamour was taken care of with the camouflage look.

RAVAGE
Menswear Forecasters, Trend Union

RAVAGE, international artist duo Clemens Rameckers and Arnold van Geuns, has specialized in fashion, textile and interiors for decades. They produce one of the most important menswear trend references (the colour book) for Trend Union, Paris.

Why menswear? During our arts school studies (at the end of the 1960s and the beginning of the 1970s), menswear little by little asserted its place under the sun. Pop music (English pop music) enormously influenced men's 'vestimentary' behaviour. Carnaby Street for the first time offered a men's wardrobe specially made for the youngsters. Tapestry, Union Jack, flower jackets, lace shirts, high-neck shirt-collars, Liberty prints, bellbottom trousers, large at the bottom and ultra tight at the belt, proudly showing men's sexual attributes.

1.24

1.24
Rameckers and van Geuns mention the Three Musketeers and paintings of Frans Hals as one of their favourite fashion moments because of the flamboyant, nonchalant and masculine nature of the subjects.

What are your favourite menswear moments of the past? Early-seventeenth-century Louis XIII (Three Musketeers, Frans Hals) – flamboyant, nonchalant, very manly. Mid-eighteenth-century Louis XV (Liaisons Dangereuses, Lace Wars) – refined, opulent, lace and brocades, very virile (second degree). Early-nineteenth-century Regency (Brummel, Pushkin) – sober, refined, very strict rules, hours in front of the mirror and spoiling the whole in a minute, very decadent. Early-twentieth-century Rich White Russians, meeting even richer American Millionaires on French Riviera. Gordon Parks 'Superfly' – very beautiful.

Who is the future of menswear (new designer hopeful)? The future of fashion is there already; bloggers and magazines make fashion. There are Fashion Weeks all over the world, all over the year; people nowadays have to see what's happening in Milan, London, Paris, New York, etc. But Berlin, Bratislava, Warsaw, St Petersburg, Amsterdam, Dublin, just to name a few, also have their Fashion Weeks; the period we live in is rather unique in history. Never has fashion, and/or the importance of being dressed, been so present/omnipresent – hysterical, even. Everybody is his own fashion designer . . . we mix, we cut, we add, with great creativity and without hang-ups. Bloggers stop us in the street, we have our moment of glory, we get followers, we start a fashion line and can become millionaires; bloggers do become millionaires also.

When we carefully scrutinize fashion – I mean men's fashion, hip fashion – we see that, in fact, very few things happen. I was talking about the very strict boundaries in which menswear is imprisoned. We still wear jackets, trousers and shirts as a base to play on. The very innovative Alexander McQueen menswear strictly holds on to these classical ingredients even with extreme ideas for menswear, with the great results we all know.

I think, but I'm afraid that it is wishful thinking, that after a long period of hip-hysterical fashion, we'll come back to a very well balanced, discreet non-fashion, non-ostentatious, so to say. This fashion exists already – I mean, the ingredients have already been there for a long time – but of course magazines have no interest in it. We can resume this idea by saying that in fact nothing is really changing in fashion, but the way to present it is continuously changing. Karl Lagerfeld's shows are a good example of it. Every season we're anxiously waiting for the show we're going to see, the fact that Chanel will continue to present 'tailleurs' we knew already. Fashion has become a very exciting show business: operas made by very talented stage designers.

What is your view on trends? First of all, let's talk about whom we are working for. We work for the fashion industry, which must deliver the ingredients with which millions of young and less young fashion professionals and fashion amateurs can make their look. We try to analyse and unknot/unloose that enormous amount of fashion information and images we see in magazines, on blogs and in the street to give to industry the information with which it can make their collections. This information is very important for designers and retailers. We are not only talking about basics, or essentials. We provide information on what is happening and how to react to it. We start with colour, the most important item of our seasonal information.

We must not forget the fashion items that magazines sell us as most important, be it unveiled male sex (Rick Owens), gender 'mixtures', outrageous make-up (Thom Brown), etc., which are rarely seen in the street.

Therefore, we have to analyse carefully what's happening, not to misinform our clients.

How can trends help a retailer? Trends help the retailer to sell clothes; we help the retailer choose which trends to focus on. We inform about shapes and silhouette changes and also for which part of the market these changes are important.

How can trends help a designer? Trends help designers to do what all the others do, and so earn money. Avant-garde, in general, is not a money machine. Apart from some very talented artists like Iris van Herpen, everybody creating fashion is turning around in the same circles. Shoe design is a very good example of this, to understand what we're talking about; very crazy and creative, but still all designed on the same shape for years already.

What is your methodology (how do you detect trends)? We do not really detect trends, but we have a fine nose for what's happening on the market and in market behaviour. 'We shop, therefore we are'; we read, we buy magazines – and not only fashion magazines. We see what's happening on the web. So much is happening nowadays that it becomes very difficult to form a proper opinion of what is going to and what is not going to become an important movement or trend. We must also not forget that we have long lasting fashions or habits and we have short trends – or even ephemeral trends or pop-ups! Trends that last one summer, for example, are less interesting for industry as a real, solid new wave that industry can surf on for several seasons or even years. We have to be very careful not to give too much attention to trends. Another difficult thing is: for what group or layer in the market are we working? We can no longer speak of menswear as one item. We have Junior, Street, City, Hipsters, Business, etc. to cope with . . . all different markets, all different timings. For example what we (Ravage) wore with pride about thirty years ago – the three-piece suit we had made in tweed or raw silk, completed with Jermyn Street shirts, and shoes – is again very much a hot item. However, we should not make the mistake of presenting this for men of our age. It's a youngster/designer item.

How long does it take to prepare a presentation? We spend a lot of time preparing our season presentations. In fact, it is an everyday discipline.

What are the most important big menswear trends for the coming years? For many different markets there will be many different trends that pop up, of course. Young designers will of course re-re-re-discover the beauty of 'Highland costume', 'Indian pageantry', 'East African tribal adornment', '1930 Chicago Gangsters', 'Cybertechnology', etc., etc. (we have seen these things pass by a thousand times in the last 40 years) . . . but the big thing will be the mixture made of all this in one silhouette. Sportswear or active sportswear will be mixed with city classics, male and female, rich and poor, baroque and sober, very big shapes and very tight slim fits, sexy and prudish, vulgar and ultra-chic, Prince and Clochard. All these things built on a long-lasting, slowly changing, unisex wardrobe that has existed already for a long time and in which young couples spent their weekends at home. For the elder generation.

CHAPTER SUMMARY

Today's world is full of multiple trends, all trying to be adopted at once, making trend forecasting a challenging and exciting process. Music, new styles and societal attitudes intermix to create new directions, but much can still be learnt from history. History has shown us how some of the main events in a society has influenced menswear and how the birth of subcultures has created elements that are still part of menswear today, albeit in a new format.

Knowing the history of trends and menswear creates a solid foundation for understanding the now and predicting the future. Previous trends are always present in one form or another, but one becomes a developing trend only when a larger group starts adopting it as fashion.

HOMEWORK ASSIGNMENTS

1. Research major historical events over the past few hundred years and look at the style of menswear of the period soon after each. Find connections and propose some possible reasons that men wore certain types of dress.
2. Look at various trend agency websites and see if you can discern the areas where each specializes. Study a paid website's free portal first, and then investigate its social media links and blogs to help further your analysis.
3. List some subcultures of today. Do they have a particular way of dressing? What do they communicate through their dress? What are the demographics and main channels of communication for these subcultures?

DISCUSSION ACTIVITIES AND PROJECTS

1. Research online what past sumptuary laws you can find for men and discuss why these laws were in place.

2. Define Dandyism further by researching in your library the lifestyles and the aesthetics of this cult of dressing.

3. What is the Dandy of today? Can you identify and define it in contemporary fashion language?

KEY WORDS
commodity
Dandy
menswear
preppie
societal
subcultures
sumptuary
trend agencies
trend analysis
trend forecasting
trends
Zeitgeist

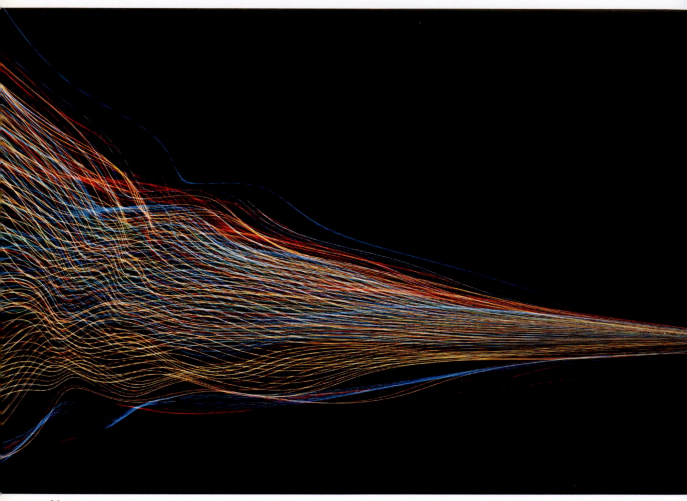

2.1

2.1
Trends are
influenced by
many factors
from society,
culture, street and
general consumer
behaviour.

2

Defining Trend Thinking and Concepts

LEARNING OBJECTIVES

- Understand the terminology used in menswear trend forecasting and analysis.
- Explore the most commonly referenced theories used as the basis for current trend thinking.
- Differentiate between trend, fashion and clothing.
- Compare the relationship between mega, macro and micro trends.
- Understand the cyclical nature of trends.
- Define early adopters, early to late majority and laggard consumers.
- Understand trend timelines in relation to fashion timelines.

INTRODUCTION

Trend prediction information is important for retailers and designers alike. Often menswear design graduates want to become trend-setting designers, which means focusing on a small sector of the market. However, the majority of menswear brands prefer to provide products that most men want – that is, that are targeted at the mainstream market. Of course, creativity cannot be removed from the process, but by taking trends into consideration it is possible to reach a commercial balance.

Trend thinking can be divided into analysis and forecasting. 'Analysis' is what is happening in the marketplace currently, and 'forecasting' is what is predicted will happen in menswear in the future.

Forecasting is often based on a 'hunch', and intuition is a good starting point. However, it is important to carry out systematic research and utilize predictive models (which will be covered in subsequent chapters), rather than just observing what is happening on catwalks at the moment. In trend prediction, it is important to consider everything from societal change to early signals in fashion.

Generally speaking, menswear trend analysis is monitoring current catwalk and retail along with street style, whereas forecasting is based on understanding fashion change, the cyclical nature of fashion and how these affect the future of menswear. Trend thinking is part analysis and part forecasting. One has to be aware of what has happened, is happening, and will happen in menswear.

Trends often arise in a general way that can then develop into a menswear-specific trend. The reverse is also true: fashion trends can be applied to many industries, from technology to hospitality. Companies that are not in the fashion industry often look at its consumer information and trend forecasts. There is so much data to be digested, and fashion forecasting filters and provides useful information for many other industries. For example, forecasting can monitor

2.2
Menswear catwalks are a focal point for press and trend forecasters alike. Here we see the Sacai S/S 2016 Paris presentation.

2.3
A typical menswear trend forecast spread that includes societal factors from art and interiors as well as fashion elements such as catwalk and editorial items.

global youth movements and cultures, advising about how this will influence the consumer of tomorrow. Colour and material forecasting can give inspirational direction to companies. Instead of just being 'inspired' by catwalks, designers in diverse industries can create stories that meet the needs of their audiences.

Some important customer behaviour theories, such as the diffusion of innovation, meme and tipping point theories, are essential in understanding the male customer. One of the most important parts of the methodology involves translating it into contemporary, practical language for the menswear consumer. This chapter's exploration of these theories includes examples that illustrate how they can be applied to today's menswear.

Intuition, research and an understanding of behaviour theories are all vital in trend prediction. It is important to develop and refine your own system in order to become a successful menswear trend specialist.

2.2

2.3

TRENDS AND FASHION

Because 'fashion' is defined as something that is adopted by a larger group of people, it is important that the term 'trend' be kept distinct. If trend behaviour becomes adopted behaviour, it becomes fashion (see Figure 2.4). Trends belong to the innovator stage and early adopter stage, whereas fashion belongs to the early and late majority stage. When it reaches the laggard stage, fashion simply becomes clothing (see the section in this chapter titled 'Personifications of Behaviour' for more on these stages).

However, the trend unit does often cross over the tipping point (see the section in this chapter titled 'Tipping Point Theory') and attach to fashions. It gives basic fashion the distinctive characteristics that differentiate clothes styles from one another.

TREND STRUCTURE

'Trend' is defined as 'a tendency towards a particular direction'. We can define a unit within this field that allows us to find the components of any given trend: a trend unit. A trend unit is a trend that is part of a bigger trend. For example, a handbag may consist of several trends: a bag size trend, an accessory component trend and a surface trend (including colour and material trends). Each of these separate trends would be the units that compose the larger bag trend. The bag can itself be part (a unit) of a bigger accessory trend. Fashion items can always be broken down into trend units, which exist throughout the evolution of a trend.

The trend unit can exist independently or within a bigger context. For example, a superstructure of trend units builds a larger trend, such as a lifestyle trend. The lifestyle trend can be composed of interiors, art, literature and fashion trends. The structure consists of framework of smaller units – trend units – that create the bigger structure. Each one of these smaller trends can be used as trend items, whereas the superstructure exists because of the multiple components.

To use the example of menswear lifestyle trends (see Figure 2.5): men are becoming more aware of the importance of exercise and sport, are more health conscious and participate more in sports. This creates a good foundation for incorporating more sport references into men's wardrobe. Trainers, college sweaters and sport-inspired items are part of the basic trend units of any *sporty* menswear trend.

Trainers are a part of this bigger lifestyle trend, but as a product, they also have trends within themselves. And just as trainers have their own trends, so do their soles. Footwear component manufacturers at trade shows often present component trends.

The list goes on. There are trends for jackets but also trends for the fabrics. For shirts, shirting manufacturers base their prints on trends; collar and even button makers do the same. A shirt is a combination of trend units that creates the whole larger structure of the shirt. A shirt is, in turn, part of the bigger trend structure. It is possible to pick any part of menswear and create a trend report for that particular element.

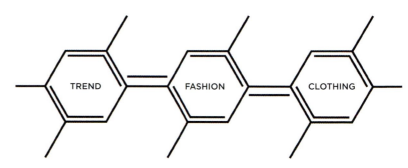

2.4

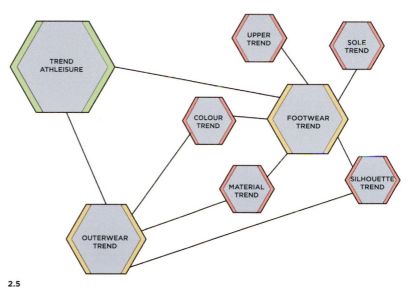

2.5

2.4
Trends evolve into fashion that will then become clothing. The full life cycle of fashion innovation can be years.

2.5
A trend can live in a bigger structure of trends, such as lifestyle, that in turn can be broken down to smaller sections of the same trend. The trend can be found in shapes, colours, surface detailing and other features, whether the product is shoes or outerwear.

THE BASICS OF TREND TIMELINES

One of the main aspects in understanding trend forecasting is timing and its relation to various seasons. The fashion cycle can be broken down into sourcing, wholesale and retail seasons. The trend industry caters to all three seasons, whether the target customer is the designer or the materials producer. In short, design houses buy materials (sourcing) to make the sales samples (wholesale) that will end up in stores next season (retail). Trend forecasting must be done six to eight months before the start of sampling (the moment when brands start making sales samples for the following season). However, trend analysis is much closer to the retail season, focusing on the fashion selling season (catwalks and trade shows) and even retail analysis.

The average production cycle for menswear is one year from a design idea to the shop and the consumer. However, the timings can depend on the size of the company and other factors, such as distribution and the specific sector of menswear (e.g., luxury, mass, sportswear). Trend forecast work is used most often before the design process; therefore, the trend information must have been gathered at least some months before the material trade shows start. Material trade shows are also a good point at which to confirm whether the forecaster is on the right track with the general moods of upcoming seasons. Trends cater to all aspects of the market, from the yarn and fibre makers to fabric producers to final product, as well as throughout the post-product life of marketing, visual merchandising and packaging of product.

2.6

2.7

PRODUCTION TIMELINE: IDEA TO PRODUCT

After the design idea is finalized, the prototyping and development will take at least six months from the purchase of raw materials. This again depends on the size of the company and distribution channels, but an average-size menswear company can turn a collection around from design idea to a fitted sellable sample in six months. After the fit, colours and labelling are completed, the sales samples are ordered for catalogues in anticipation of the selling season.

The design process starts long before the final retail product is available; this can be several months, depending on the design team. The time frame from idea to product is approximately eight to ten months; from idea to retail

2.6
Designers go to sourcing trade shows with their inspirational ideas to look for materials for sampling.

2.7
Material manufacturers can take years to develop new finishes and items to show in trade shows.

is approximately fourteen to sixteen months. Designers and design houses should go to the materials shows with finished designs – or at least initial design ideas. The materials sourcing shows are very trend driven, with specific 'trend areas' giving designers direction, while helping and inspiring the material buying process.

BUYING TIMELINE: PRODUCT TO SHOP

Once the collection is ready to be shown at a trade show, showroom or catwalk, the journey of the product to retail starts. The retail-selling season in menswear starts in January for the following autumn/winter and in June for the following spring/summer. Deliveries of final goods greatly depend on the agreement between the designer/brand and the retailer. Generally speaking, the production of goods has to start within a month or two after the order is confirmed. Therefore, the brand will have about six months from the first viewing of the product (e.g., at a trade show) to the completion of the order. For example, most product orders will be written in January when a brand presents its collections to a buyer in an autumn/winter trade show or showroom. Within weeks after the show, the brand will send a pro-forma invoice to the buyer to confirm the order.

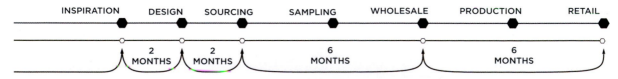

2.8

After all the orders are in, the brand will then start production around March. For average-size menswear companies, the delivery of goods is usually around September. Several bigger menswear companies, such as Hilfiger, already have their winter collections coming in as early as July. However, the average timing from first presentation of the product to arriving on the shop floor is about six months. The same cycle and timing repeats for spring/summer orders. Trade shows occur around June and order confirmations around July, with store deliveries in January.

The first opportunity to see menswear of the new season is with London Collections Men, soon followed by Florence's Pitti Uomo. Both shows kick off the season. Subsequently, Milan, Paris and New York menswear shows round out the season. There are numerous other shows that surround the buying season, which we review in more detail on page 150. Although menswear shows start before womenswear shows, the menswear selling can continue in parallel with the womenswear season. The bulk of menswear buying is done in the month after the opening of the season, but casual and streetwear brands are continuing to show together with womenswear. These include the main shoe and accessories shows that also offer men's collections.

2.9

2.8
The full design cycle – from inspiration to final retail product – is on average sixteen months.

2.9
Retail is the end of the journey for the design process, but the start of marketing and retail analysis. Prada space in Aoyama, Tokyo, Japan.

WATER STAINS   RAW COAST

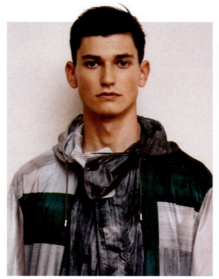

SPRING / SUMMER 17   **FASHION**SNOOPS

2.10

2.10
Trend companies also offer early mood references, especially for materials and colour, as seen here by Fashion Snoops.

2.11
While researching trends, consider the production timeline. For example, if trend research is done for a raw materials manufacturer, the work will have to be done several months before the product is due to retail. The graph above is a general guideline on what to research during which season.

TREND FORECASTING TIMELINE: CULTURE TO RETAIL

Trend forecasting has to start very early to be able to offer companies enough time to apply the information to their product and strategy. Consider that the materials trade shows (which show one year before the retail season) also use trend services. They need trend information a minimum of four to six months before their production, which means the forecaster works on the information (such as colour) six to eight months before that production date. Trend forecasting for materials producers is among the earliest types of forecasting for fashion.

Because menswear presentations are earlier, their forecasts must also be done earlier. Various seasons are worked on simultaneously; while a presentation is finished for one season, research for another has started. Exact timing for a cultural starting point of a trend is more difficult to pinpoint. Early signals, such as early innovations from culture, can manifest in the way we dress quite rapidly, but they may also take years to develop. For example, material innovation can translate to finished product quickly (antibacterial, breathable fabrics) or it can take longer to be adopted (Hussein Chalayan's self-zipping dresses). When working with trends, we do need to be clear about what can be applied in a product and what is more visionary.

ANALYSIS TIMELINE: FROM RUNWAY TO FAST FASHION

Trends analysis concerns itself with menswear trends that are already manifesting strongly in society, especially on catwalks and on streets. Street styling is not new, but it has evolved into a different phenomenon in the digital age. Street styling has brought a new democracy to menswear and to the fashion system. Anyone can become a trendsetter; this needs to be taken into consideration now.

Fashion shows have become exactly what the term implies: 'shows' that are a total experience, from entrance to runway walks to front row media coverage to back stage reporting. In our digital age, we often receive reports from back stage even before the show takes place. We can follow designers' and creative directors' social media accounts to get an idea of a collection's themes before it has even been designed.

We should take all the available details into consideration. In order to make a full catwalk analysis, we must include more depth, moving beyond reporting what was seen on the runways. A good trend analysis not only describes what trends are manifesting on the catwalk but also why. This brings a greater margin of usefulness to the analysis than is found in the ubiquitous and rather superficial reporting offered by the endless number of self-made online fashion specialists.

Catwalk analysis is also a good moment for the forecaster to reflect on and validate his or her vision in previous forecasts. Commercial fashion publications want and need trend analysis, and it helps trends to become mainstream fashion.

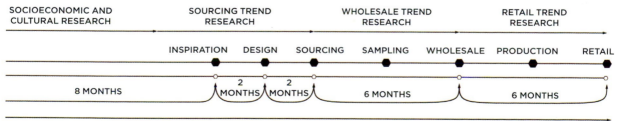

SOCIOECONOMIC AND CULTURAL RESEARCH | SOURCING TREND RESEARCH | WHOLESALE TREND RESEARCH | RETAIL TREND RESEARCH

INSPIRATION   DESIGN   SOURCING   SAMPLING   WHOLESALE   PRODUCTION   RETAIL

8 MONTHS | 2 MONTHS | 2 MONTHS | 6 MONTHS | 6 MONTHS

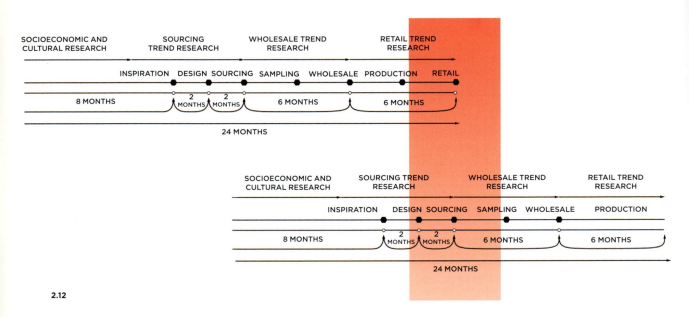

SOCIOECONOMIC AND CULTURAL RESEARCH

SOURCING TREND RESEARCH

WHOLESALE TREND RESEARCH

RETAIL TREND RESEARCH

INSPIRATION   DESIGN   SOURCING   SAMPLING   WHOLESALE   PRODUCTION   RETAIL

8 MONTHS   2 MONTHS   2 MONTHS   6 MONTHS   6 MONTHS

24 MONTHS

SOCIOECONOMIC AND CULTURAL RESEARCH

SOURCING TREND RESEARCH

WHOLESALE TREND RESEARCH

RETAIL TREND RESEARCH

INSPIRATION   DESIGN   SOURCING   SAMPLING   WHOLESALE   PRODUCTION

8 MONTHS   2 MONTHS   2 MONTHS   6 MONTHS   6 MONTHS

24 MONTHS

2.12

2.12
The coloured highlight represents the busy overlapping of seasons. When working with trends, forecasters are often working and researching several seasons at once.

DIFFUSION OF INNOVATIONS

Everett M. Rogers' *Diffusion of Innovations* offers perhaps the most important research model used in trends and trend forecasting. This theory from 1962 explains how innovation is adopted and spreads through a community at the same rate, regardless of culture and type of community.

PERSONIFICATIONS OF BEHAVIOUR

The book's main premise is that an idea introduced to society may diffuse by regular patterns, influenced by four main elements (i.e., the innovation itself, communication channels, time and a social system).

Rogers also identified types of people relating to the idea and its adoption. There are five personifications of behaviour, including *innovators, early adopters, early majority, late majority* and *laggards*. The innovators are the ones who actually introduce the idea to society, 'launching the new idea in the system by importing the innovation from outside of the system's boundaries. Thus, the innovator plays a gatekeeping role in the flow of new ideas into the system' (Rogers 2003: 283). Innovators are usually risk-taking, venturesome, cosmopolitan and the most creative of all groups, comprising 2.5 per cent of society.

The next group after the innovators is the *early adopters*. This group makes a great subject for trend forecasting practice, since most trends are initially recognizable in this group. They are locally connected but use social media to reach an audience while being the strongest opinion leaders. *Early adopters* are considered role models and are the ones who approve the new innovations in society that are introduced by the innovators.

The next group, *early majority*, looks to the *early adopters* as a test group before approving the innovation. Since early majority is a large portion of society, 34 per cent, this forms an important target group for the fashion business. The early majority people are willing to take on new ideas but seldom lead with innovation. They are not the first to try an idea – but not the last ones, either.

The next group is called the *late majority*, also 34 per cent, who are the most sceptical of all the groups. They usually adopt due to economic or peer pressures. Any uncertainty about a new idea must dissipate before it reaches the *late majority*. After the innovation has passed through the *late majority*, it reaches the traditionalists, also known as *laggards*. The *laggards* are suspicious of all innovations and changes; they take no initiative and have no opinion leadership. They are the last to adopt an idea and often do it only when no other options are available.

The *Diffusion of Innovation* theory is a complex one, but in this simplified form it provides a good basic platform for trend prediction analysis.

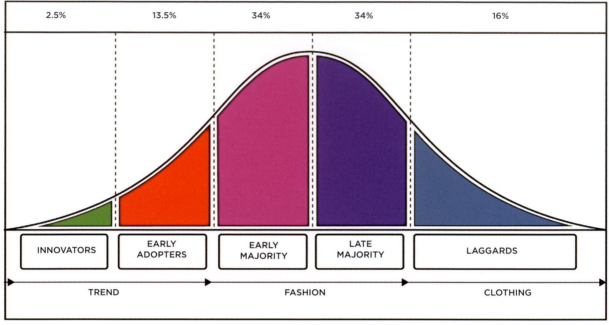

| 2.5% | 13.5% | 34% | 34% | 16% |

| INNOVATORS | EARLY ADOPTERS | EARLY MAJORITY | LATE MAJORITY | LAGGARDS |

TREND — FASHION — CLOTHING

2.13

2.13
Diffusion of innovation bell shows how innovation travels through society.

2.14
Henrik Vibskov is very much an innovator in the world of menswear, introducing innovative materials, colour and styling for men. S/S 2015 Paris.

MENSWEAR DIFFUSION OF INNOVATION

Rogers' diffusion of innovation theory can be applied to menswear. The categories he identified can be identified today in menswear consumers: innovators, early adopters, early majority, late majority and laggards.

Innovators would be the designers who introduce a new idea or style that is not prevailing fashion at the moment. Today, designers such as J. W. Anderson and Henrik Vibskov would fit this category well, since they introduce new ideas to menswear audiences. Another innovator in today's menswear market is Thom Browne. He is constantly presenting ideas that are not only new in menswear, but also innovative.

Fashion graduate designers are often innovative thinkers as well; they can use their creativity to the fullest and not worry about the commercial risk involved. Outside of the actual fashion business of material or silhouette innovations, innovators can also be muses and style icons for menswear. Even a celebrity can be a vehicle of innovation, as was the case with David Beckham. He was the face of the 'metrosexual' male trend when it was introduced. Writer and journalist Mark Simpson invented the term in 1994, but it really did not become a global phenomenon until the concept was introduced to a wider audience in 2002 with David Beckham (Simpson 2002).

Innovators can also be men who are photographed

in street-style shots. These men, the *flâneurs* or peacock dressers of the contemporary fashion system, are often seen outside the catwalk and trade shows. Some simply dress in an interesting way; some wear innovative outfits in hopes of getting photographed. The street-style shot has become another venue for presenting new ideas to the system.

Early adopters are men who are the first to wear the styles recently introduced; they are confident fashion opinion leaders. The early adopters usually have the financial stability to experiment with new ideas without great risk, allowing them to quickly adopt fashion changes. In today's world the Internet has provided a whole new venue for spreading influence and seeking approval. Bloggers are a good example. They can be innovators, in some cases, but often they exploit new designer products as early adopters. However, you do not have to be a fashion blogger to be an early adopter. The Internet has simply provided another platform for pushing innovation forward. After a certain look is adopted, accepted and widely available in the marketplace, then the early majority will buy into the innovation or the menswear style. Early majority menswear consumers need to have seen the product move through the approval stage before committing to it. This is the first part of fashion becoming mainstream. It is this moment – when trends evolve into

mainstream – that a forecaster needs to predict. When a trend reaches this point, it becomes 'bankable'.

The following 34 per cent of the population (i.e., the late majority) consists of the mainstream menswear consumer, who adopts a look once it is a prevailing style in the system. This means the fashion

2.14

2.15

is well on its way to becoming a mainstream phenomenon, and this is the point at which it peaks and then begins its decline. This is the stage at which a menswear trend starts to lose its fashion appeal.

The last stage and the last group to buy menswear are the laggards, who buy in when the trend has lost most of its fashion clout and has become simply clothing. Laggards often adopt the style when there is either no other option or when it raises the least attention.

But how does one use this information in trend forecasting? The services that a forecaster is selling are, first, the ability to understand where trends develop from and, second, the foresight to determine which early trend signals are likely to develop into current trends. Therefore, understanding the early stages is vital, especially for designers who would like to design menswear that men will want.

The early majority is a reference point to see what is currently in store and selling. This information can be used in merchandising and strategic retail trend thinking. When a trend has evolved into the retail mainstream, it is too late to use the information to improve actual collections. This needs to be done at the innovation stage for fashion designers and directional brands (e.g., brands that are more risk-taking, such as Opening Ceremony or Vetements). For mainstream fashion houses (e.g., Calvin Klein, Tommy Hilfiger), the information reference point is at the early adopters stage.

Rogers' diffusion of innovation theory has been applied here in a very broad sense, but it can be a very valuable tool for analyzing contemporary menswear behaviour.

2.15
Thom Browne has become the new trendsetter for menswear with his show-stopping presentations. S/S 2017 Paris.

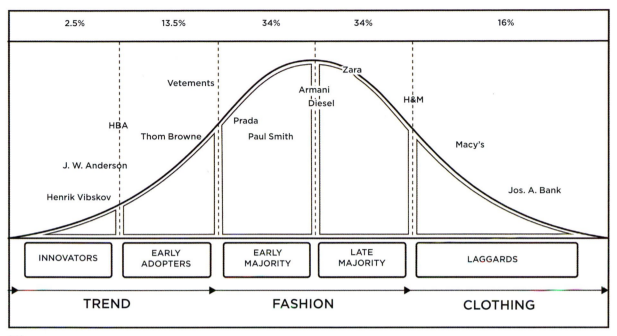

| 2.5% | 13.5% | 34% | 34% | 16% |

Vetements

Zara

Armani
Diesel

HBA

H&M

Prada

Thom Browne

Paul Smith

J. W. Anderson

Macy's

Henrik Vibskov

Jos. A. Bank

| INNOVATORS | EARLY ADOPTERS | EARLY MAJORITY | LATE MAJORITY | LAGGARDS |

TREND   FASHION   CLOTHING

2.16

2.16
In this menswear diffusion of innovation curve, it is possible to see where a contemporary brand would be placed.

TIPPING POINT THEORY

The term 'tipping point' is broadly defined as the moment when an idea crosses a threshold to become widespread and accepted. The term is often used in economic and popular culture to describe a triggering moment when something gains substantial momentum or becomes a bigger phenomenon.

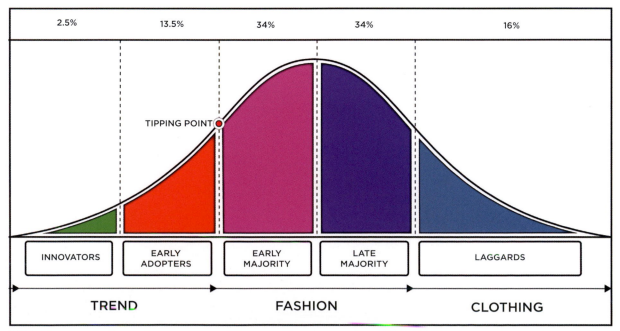

TREND TIPPING POINT

The term was used to describe a sociological phenomenon by Morton Grodzins in his 1957 *Scientific American* article and his later book. The phrase became a global buzz phrase in the year 2000, when Malcolm Gladwell analysed this popularly used term within the context of trends (in his book *The Tipping Point: How Little Things Can Make a Big Difference*).

In trend forecasting we determine when a trend will probably pass the tipping point to become a widely accepted idea. In menswear we find many examples: skinny jeans, Barbour jackets and Adidas plastic slider slippers. Each started as an early signal that gained momentum, reaching a point where it became mainstream fashion. Almost all will eventually taper off until they are seen rarely, if at all. Only a few will have enough staying power to become classics.

The question is how to predict whether and when these transitions will happen. According to Gladwell's book, one key aspect of trends is their 'stickiness factor' – in other words, how catchy the trend is, what unique characteristics can be identified at first and, above all, who the early adopters of the idea are. If these factors appear strong, the trend will most likely reach a tipping point.

2.17
The tipping point in fashion occurs when a trend 'tips' over a certain number of wearers to become something that is adopted by the larger group (i.e., the trend becomes fashion).

2.18
Beards reached the tipping point in 2014–15 and have now reached early/late majority. Hair trends, whether facial or head, take years to go in and out of fashion.

2.18

MEME THEORY

Richard Dawkins writes about human behaviour. In his book *The Selfish Gene* (1976/2006), he introduces the word 'meme', which he defines as a behaviour that is passed on from person to person through imitation and replication.

MEMES AND MENSWEAR

Dawkins says, 'Examples of memes are tunes, ideas, catch-phrases, clothes fashions, ways of making pots or of building arches' (Dawkins 1976/2006: 192). We might conclude that all of menswear is memes: information that one person imitates after seeing another person. Some fashion memes are better than others and are copied more, spreading the meme further.

According to Dawkins, a meme's high survival rate depends on its longevity, fecundity and copying-fidelity. Longevity of a meme simply means that it has some lasting power to go through the full life cycle and not suffer premature death. In menswear, classics are memes that have longevity. Fecundity means that the meme (for example, a type of shoes) must be copied numerous times, and copying-fidelity means the meme is copied accurately. When the meme or the fashion is copied with variations and differences, it evolves and becomes another meme. Dawkins calls this a type of behavioural evolution.

The meme theory has been taken further by many other analysts, but Dawkins' theory provides a good guideline to understanding the process of how information is replicated and copied from person to person. We learn behaviour through imitation from our parents (memetic vertical flow) and from peers and people outside the family (memetic horizontal flow). A meme can also be stored in history, appear again, be adopted and gain momentum – a complex process to stay aware of when analyzing menswear trends.

The basic premises of meme theory allow us to more clearly understand menswear consumer behaviour and the importance of imitation in fashion.

2.19

2.19
Trade shows such
as Pitti Uomo are
where memes begin
trying to catch on
and compete to
become the next
big trend.

INTUITIVE APPROACH

Intuition is often dismissed as a form of methodology because it is not based on logic or rational thinking. The main reason for this dismissal is that intuition cannot be measured and verified. Yet we all occasionally have a gut feeling or a hunch and often use it as the sole basis for impulse decisions. As Li Edelkoort, the world's leading trend forecaster, says: 'Intuition is like a muscle; it gets stronger the more you use it' (personal conversation, Italy, 2012).

An intuitive approach is perhaps the most difficult to measure because it is based on a personal ability to make judgements and predictive associations based on a hunch or a feeling. However, most trend professionals agree that in the prediction process selection is based on this intuitive ability to group things together. The intuitive approach also provides a project signature and a personal touch.

The most important part of intuition is having the confidence to trust it. We are composed of experiences and various learned and imitated behaviours, including the way we dress. One of the foundations of intuition is learning to sense the environment and the world around you. Based on these observations, you can draw conclusions and learn to envision future behavioural directions.

It is a good idea to start forecasting with a clear mental space of silent solitude and your personal operating system – the brain – rather than by reading magazines and scanning social media, which will be the second stage of the system. Goodiepal, an experimental musician, says that the world is full of quotes, and people are endlessly quoting other people's ideas because original thinking no longer exists (Andersen 2012: 11). This might be true; our minds are primarily composed of information that we have absorbed from various sources. It is nearly impossible today to be cut off from other people and technology for substantial lengths of time. We are living in a symbiosis, or perhaps a parasitic relationship, with new media and technology.

Let your own mind guide your direction sometimes, without the distractions of all the electronic information around you. In other words, let your brain, rather than the technology, do the initial thinking. There are intuitive exercises at the end of this chapter that will help you to focus and trust your intuitive sense.

FASHION CHANGE AND CYCLE

Menswear fashion change is slower than womenswear, but it is gaining momentum as men want greater seasonal variety and are starting to express themselves more through their outfits. In order to gain a deeper understanding of menswear behaviour, a more profound review of culture is required.

COMMUNICATION AND MENSWEAR

Fashion has been extensively studied and written about as cultural phenomena. Historically, it usually focused on dress as a way of communicating financial or social status. However, in modern society the communication of status may not be as relevant to fashion as it once was; the expensive made-to-measure suit or pair of shoes may not be as much about status as the new car or latest technological device is. Although some men spend money on clothes to compete, which drives a trend forward, that is not necessarily the case for all.

In today's social media game, appearances are everything. The image has overtaken text and opinion feeds. The evolution of social media has moved from LiveJournal, which was very much about writing, to Facebook, which is more about short statements, to Instagram, which is image/video based, to Snapchat, where messages have to be viewed in an instant and cannot be saved. Communication through images has become the most important channel for men, influencing spending and appearance. For example, in Instagram there are millions of hashtags that reference menswear or the 'outfit of the day'. The men of today do not necessarily flaunt the ability to buy something, but rather communicate their early adopter status. Early adoption has become the desired status in fashion, including in menswear.

TREND CYCLES

Most trends are around all the time. Some trends bubble under and vibrate a little stronger than others, manifesting as a stronger movement.

A trend forecaster needs to tap into this and understand the cyclical nature of trends. Trends do not go in a circle but rather in a spiral, constantly manifesting themselves in a slightly different format. It is not so easy to follow all the changes of the cycles, but there certainly is a pattern in such easily detectable details as colour, silhouette and trouser width/length. Some styles take five years to return, others might even take centuries. A trend initially is just a signal (innovation); once it has gained some momentum (early adoption) it will become a recognizable (tipping point) sound that will be embraced by the majority of a given group, reaching the peak of the trend. When the trend reaches the mainstream, it becomes fashion, the consumed end-product. After this, it fades away, and other signals will replace it until

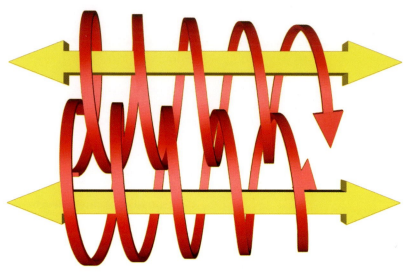

2.20

it is time for it to come back again in a slightly new format.

The shape of jeans is a good example for observing the trend cycle. The 1970s saw bell bottoms with very low-hung, super-tight denim. In the mid-1970s the leg had become more narrow with a Punk influence. By the late 1980s there was an emerging Rave culture that supported the super wide elephant denim leg, a variation of the bell bottom from ten years earlier. Jeans through the 1990s ended up narrower, with the 2000s reaching the super skinny denim for men that has again lasted for ten years.

Most trends always exist, but they 'fade in' and 'fade out' systematically as they spiral around, never resurfacing exactly the same – perhaps because everything around us is evolving as well. When trends resurface they come back in a slightly different format. Camouflage, for

example, has become a basic menswear pattern, a classic, and its popularity comes in spiral-like cycles, manifesting differently each time. During the early turn of the millennium, when camouflage started to come into menswear very strongly, brands such as the UK's Maharishi showed it in a traditional yet updated use, and Bape from Japan brought colour and new playful influences to the military pattern.

In today's world you can see camouflage in every aspect of menswear, from shoes and undergarments to suits. Even when camouflage 'peaks' and then its variations fade away, the standard military camouflage stays and continues as a basic pattern. Recently, we have seen camouflage so much in every season that its creative variations have now gone into dormancy for a while. The standard camouflage has simply become a menswear

2.20
Trend spiral: trends may come back after a certain time, but they are never completely the same, simply because times change and trends adapt. The movement is spiral rather than circular.

staple. How or when will a new camouflage peak again? It is often the case that army themes come back to catwalks and retail when there is international military conflict, suggesting that the influence of news, information and images of world events is far-reaching.

fashion will not be formed – its sway will abruptly end.' The cycles of spirals spin with their own pulse, their endless ideas intertwining, making the world of trends what it is: one of the most dynamic and interesting aspects of fashion culture.

COUNTER TRENDS

Counter trends are not the opposite of trends but really simply a trend that appears to be the opposite of a trend that has become the prevailing fashion of the moment. Many larger companies that are considered trend setting subscribe to trend services and look for what not to do, rather than which trends to follow. Counter trends are a reaction to the moment. To put it simply, if everyone in the fashion system is doing the same thing, innovators and early adaptors will do just the opposite in order to create something new. This propels fashion trends. For example, if pointy shoes have reached a majority (as we saw around 2005), as a reaction the more directional brands will produce some rounded toes. Fashion needs this constant battle to move forward, fuelled by the duality.

The concept was analysed by the German sociologist Georg Simmel as early as 1904 in his essential article, 'Fashion': 'Two social tendencies are essential to the establishment of fashion, namely, the need of union on the one hand and the need of isolation on the other. Should one of these be absent,

2.21

2.21
Camouflage goes through various versions and adaptations, becoming a staple surface design for menswear.

MENSWEAR ANALYSIS AND FORECASTING

Fashion trends as a business can be divided, as was done in the 'Timeline' sections in this chapter, into two distinct fields: analysis and forecasting. Trend analysis focuses on the current season, whereas trend forecasting is the predictive aspect of the trends business, developing foresight beyond the next few seasons. Both trend analysis and forecasting take cues from the catwalk, street styling, social media and print.

Trend analysis requires monitoring what is happening in fashion at the moment, dissecting that information, and explaining the state of the market. Forecasting uses this information as a starting point to predict what direction menswear will take. Both types of trend work are important for guiding companies, designers and retailers to be more 'on trend' so they can make a product that people will want.

The most distinctive difference between forecasting and analysis is the end user. Analysis is mainly geared towards the consumer. Because the analyst presents information about what is happening either at the moment or in the next season, the audience is consumers who want guidance about purchasing products. The corporate customer for this type of trend work is a retail buyer, who can gain some buying direction for the following season. The fashion-conscious media reader is the second main audience interested in this type of trend reporting. Magazines, newspapers and online media are the main portals for this.

Trend forecasting, on the other hand, happens several seasons before the goods are in stores and is mainly geared toward corporate needs: raw material production, brand sample development, line builders, collection developers, designers and so on. The menswear industry wants to make an educated guess, with the help of trend forecasting, about what men will desire and buy.

The role of the forecaster in trend forecasting and analysis is to become a strategic partner and an educator, guiding clients in the right direction and hopefully inspiring them to incorporate trend storytelling into their business module. Storytelling helps companies translate sometimes hard-to-grasp trend concepts into their corporate strategy. An example is athleisure (a trend that combines workout/athletic features into casual wear); it is used by companies in advertising campaigns, enticing the end consumer to buy into the trend story.

Ideally, the trend forecaster helps companies not to copy catwalks, but to understand the Zeitgeist, or the spirit of the times, and use their research skills to create something of their own.

TREND FORECASTING

Forecasting involves the multifaceted research of society and culture. Many societal changes trigger trends and push behaviour in a certain direction. For example, the social acceptance of sportswear for most situations has influenced the direction of menswear. Climate change, along with men travelling more frequently, has influenced menswear by blurring traditional seasonal notions, such as colour and construction.

As a forecaster, you anticipate the direction the cultural and natural forces will take. A fashion forecaster will have to research past seasons, both on the catwalk and in the culture, to see where new trends may start to develop. Forecasting is generally done at least twelve months before the wholesale season and eighteen months before the items are due to be in store.

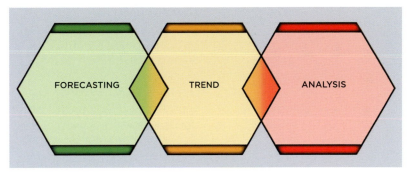

2.22

TREND ANALYSIS

Trend analysis is carried out closer to season and generally focuses on catwalk or street-style research. It is analysis of the 'now' and the possibilities that come with it. The analyst looks at directional fashion, forward-thinking editorials, street styling and catwalks to help guide buyers' menswear purchases. Catwalk analysis is useful for fashion media presenting the latest menswear concepts. Of course, it is also a huge source of 'inspiration' for fast fashion companies. It is the responsibility of the trend analyst not only to present and explain what is happening on the catwalks, but also to explain why certain trends are arising. Trend analysis is not only for product; it is also used for art directing, packaging, advertising, branding, visual merchandising and simply understanding the emotional mood of society.

2.22
Trend work can be divided into two distinct types: forecasting and analysis.

Trend Drivers

Trend drivers are elements that push the trend forward – in other words, cause the trend to gain momentum. One trend creates an environment for another trend to flourish. For example, men are taking care of their appearance more, buying and using more clothing and grooming products. One of the drivers for this trend is men's increased online visibility, thanks to social media. That's an example of a technology trend driving a large-scale fashion trend.

However, trend drivers can be from within fashion, also. The new shorter length of trouser exposes the ankle, which in turn drives colourful socks to become more popular. In this instance, one menswear trend is driving another menswear trend.

TREND TIMESPAN

Trends can be broken down into long-term (mega), intermediate (macro) or short-term (micro) trends. Fads are momentary 'crazes' that fade in and out in a matter of months.

Mega Trends

Time frame: Decades
Mega trends are very large, fundamental changes in society that influence changes in fashion. For example, political change caused the direction of men's fashion to change in the late 1700s. France's ostentatious dressing went out of vogue because of its associations with the doomed royal court. Another fundamental change in menswear throughout the twentieth century and into the twenty-first has been increasing emphasis on comfort, reflecting the new travel, leisure, and sport activities of these times. One of the biggest mega trends in recent decades is the Internet and how it has changed how we notice and experience fashion. Trends influence all aspects of menswear – not only individual garments but also the full experience of menswear, including branding, presentation and communication.

Macro Trends

Time frame: Years
A macro trend is a large-scale shift in current behaviour or attitude that will result in a trend that influences future behaviour and consumption. Interest in nature pursuits and outdoor activities that vary from camping to festivals

2.23

results in heritage fashions with an outdoor influence (e.g., tweeds, waxed jackets and caps). Subcultural influences, such as Punk, for example, have brought completely new fashion innovations to society, including frayed jeans and advances in hair gel. Increasing nomadic attitudes result in clothing that is easier to care for and adaptable. Global awareness of sustainability and climate change influences materials chosen and also encourages multi-use aspects of menswear, such as removable linings.

The majority of trends forecast today start at macro level, which then manifests at runways and at retail level.

Micro Trends

Time frame: Seasons
Micro trends are close-to-seasonal trends that are very much influenced by what is happening at the moment and are adopted quickly. These are fast-paced ideas that come and go within a few seasons and quickly dissolve, leaving room for the next idea. Fast fashion and the Internet are the drivers for these quick-moving trends that usually are more about surface than about silhouette. Items that are quicker to produce – for example, T-shirt graphics – can react quickly to what men want. Celebrity and popular culture is an important driver of this type of trend.

Fads

A fad can be defined as a trend that gains popularity very quickly and never reaches the fashion adaptation stage (i.e., when trends become fashion). We live in a fast society that is the perfect environment for fads. A fad can even occasionally skip the early adopter stage and jump into mass consumption from the initial 'craze' stage.

Today's social media is a major way these momentary trends gain global momentum quickly and go out of favour equally quickly. Many games (for example, Farmville, followed by Draw Something, followed by Candy Crush, followed by Pokémon Go), phrases and buzzwords gain fad momentum (e.g., 'swag' and 'just saying'). The plastic pool slider shoe, worn with or without socks, began as a fad and became a more widely accepted trend. Whether it will develop into something with more fashion staying power is yet to be seen. Crocs are a similar example. Fads in fashion are often cheap, colourful and easily available, thereby saturating the market very quickly.

2.24

2.23
The trouser length trend is driving the trend of colourful socks.

2.24
Beards decorated with flowers was a momentary fad driven by the Internet. Here at Coachella, a breeding ground for fads, a festival-goer is decorated with colourful flowers.

2.25

2.25
Sport slides with or
without sport logo
socks became a
fad that has slowly
evolved into various
sock/sandal trends.

2.26
Ankledana: some
fads last for a
fleeting moment.

2.26

This exercise should be done in writing, as homework.

Step 1: Intuition
Look for a quiet space, preferably a comfortable chair with good lighting. Leave all technology (including mobile phones and tablets) in another space. Do not even leave the phone in your pocket. Arm yourself with paper and a pen and think about what you have experienced lately: a story heard, a book read, a trip taken, a conversation had or a news item seen. Let your mind wander freely.

Write the keywords or phrases that come to your mind. Do not leave the space until you have twenty entries, at the very least.

Once you have reached your goal, review the ideas. Look for a pattern. See if there is something that triggers a reaction – a hunch, a feeling, an intuition. You are tapping into the subconscious to find a trend direction for further research.

Conclude your personal brainstorming and make a decision on what to research next. Write a paragraph or two about where you will pursue research on this trend. First, write a paragraph summarizing the various signals you wrote as keywords. Select the strongest direction and elaborate with your own words what type of research this will encourage you to do and how you will do it. End by giving your trend a name. This one-page essay is a road map for how to support your intuitive starting point.

Step 2: Validation
Once you have chosen your intuitive starting point, you need to look for validation.

Validation simply means that you find evidence to support your intuition-triggered trend once you start researching it. Your research should encompass all areas of media and culture, including news, magazines, exhibitions, subcultures and so on. The validation stage should include a mixture of primary sources that you gather and create yourself through an active process (photography, original data collection) and secondary sources (bringing in information that is gathered and created by someone else). Look for items that support your 'hunch'.

If the validation does not start to appear in various sources, the intuition is possibly wrong. This is when you should go back to the other intuitive signals you have gathered.

Write a small essay on this validation experience. Write an introductory paragraph that describes the trend you have intuited. Then write a paragraph that describes each of the major sources of validation you have found to support your trend.

2.27

JAANA JÄTYRI,
CEO, Trendstop

Jaana Jätyri founded Trendstop in 2002. She is a creative visionary who has worked in the trend forecasting industry for almost two decades. Throughout her career, she has pioneered reliable trend validation methods and hands-on concept-to-product translation that resonates with each client's unique target audience.

What was your first 'connection' with trends? When I was young, I thought I would become a fashion designer. I had several stylish great aunts who had worked as seamstresses or with textiles, and my sisters and I were always surrounded by the craft of making clothes. I vividly remember a TV series back in the 1980s presenting the work of top Parisian designers like Jean-Paul Gaultier and Azzedine Alaïa, and I fell in love with fashion design. At nineteen, I moved to London to study fashion at Central St Martins College of Art & Design (because by then street style was important, and London had the coolest street style). The Internet barely existed back then, and the trend forecasting industry wasn't known about in the same way as today. I first learnt of trend forecasting as a profession when my tutor selected me to work on a trend research project for the UK retailer New Look's marketing department.

What made you start your own company? During my industry placement year, as well as learning at the Victoria and Albert Museum's fashion and textile department and Savile Row tailors Gieves & Hawkes, I wanted to learn about digital fashion. I applied to work with a fashion PDM (later PLM) software company, who were the providers of fashion industry design software at the time, before Adobe Illustrator and Photoshop developed. I was trained on the software and sent to high street retailers' offices to train their designers how to use it. Designers were struggling to work with the new technology, and in addition to training, I helped them create digital design libraries to give them pre-made basic designs. After I graduated in the late 1990s, I set up a digital design consultancy to offer pre-created CAD design libraries to companies as a time-saving tool. My first clients were Marks and Spencer and River Island. The designers I was working with began asking for shapes anticipating the next season, and I started creating CAD drawings based on the latest catwalk looks. Due to increasing demand, I continued developing the trend research and forward analysis, and in 2002 Trendstop.com was launched as a global online trend service.

Can you tell us more about Trendstop? Trendstop is the first creative agency to combine a global online trend research platform with a full service design studio, range building and communications' consultancy.

2.27
Jaana Jätyri is the CEO and creative director of London-based Trendstop.

2.28

We believe that great products start from an inspired idea, followed by a successful execution. At Trendstop, we help our clients perfect this process. Our expertise is in helping clients translate trend concepts into best-selling products and enticing campaigns, while our unique validation methodology provides them with confidence to commit to trends ahead of competition.

Our agency services include creative direction, design development, strategic range building and on-trend communication. We deliver our information through workshops, hands-on sessions, live briefings, specialist trend reports and online trend memberships.

My team and I have worked with many leading retailers, brands and fashion suppliers to help introduce better trend validation and trend translation to fulfil their creative and commercial objectives.

How do you predict trends? Do you have a system? Over the past decade I have pioneered a unique methodology for deciphering trend lifecycles accurately. My team and I track emerging trends at their innovator and early adopter levels. Through our knowledge of trend innovator behaviour, we are able to project a given trend's most likely trajectory over its lifecycle through mainstream consumer groups.

Understanding the consumer mindset is key to commercial trend success.

Based on my fifteen years of experience analyzing trend cycles and observing the retail floor, I developed a process capable of identifying a trend's most appropriate mainstream translation from the consumer appeal perspective and estimate its timing more accurately than traditional forms of trend forecasting or sales data analysis.

Once I understood the mechanics of a trend, it was a small step by comparison to integrate this trend intelligence into an organization's business practices effectively.

2.28
Trendstop covers menswear alongside womenswear, systematically specializing in close-to-season analysis.

2.29
Colour language is important in menswear trend reporting, as seen here in Trendstop studios.

2.29

What is your menswear offer? At Trendstop we offer one of the leading trend forecasting services for menswear. Our forecast themes are deeply linked to early consumer micro and macro trend influences. They paint a visual picture of the consumer's aspirational mindset. Our catwalk and trade show overviews provide vital and relatable seasonal trend

2.30

knowledge across the menswear industry. From our global research and analysis, we develop our focused seasonal colour palettes, patterns, materials, key shapes and detailing forecasts for apparel, accessories and footwear. Our reliable trend validations allow brands, retailers, suppliers and agencies to react to trends at the right times for their customers.

Many trend forecasters still believe that menswear is driven by mainstream casual and formal wear. At Trendstop we recognize that newness in menswear stems from more creatively driven aspects, including a combination of new silhouettes and subtle inspirations from the women's market. As this trend continues to develop further, each season Trendstop's directional vision is increasingly relevant.

How does trend forecasting work with different level of clients? Traditionally trend forecasting services have not altered their offering to suit different markets. Yet, there is such a wide variety of different consumer types today, each responding to trends differently. At Trendstop, we study the global trend consumer 24/7. We believe we know what they will want next. We follow trend lifecycles through different consumer groups and identify the most appropriate translation and timing for a particular target audience. We customize our services so that clients are able to present and time trends appropriately for their consumer. The reliability of our work is proven in increased sales and reduced markdowns for our clients.

What is the future of trend forecasting? I believe that trend forecasting needs to become more relevant to serve today's unpredictable consumer mindset and fast-paced market. As the trend forecasting industry is not regulated, anyone is able to set themselves up as a commentator and access free global distribution of their views online. As a result, there seem to be as many 'trends' being cited as there are sources. Many even conflict with each other. Some are correct – some of the time. Unfortunately, if the advice given is not good, or if it is not followed in the right way, the resulting products or campaigns won't sell. I envisage trend analysis moving from a mostly creative focus to incorporate an aspect of commercial responsibility, so that clients are able to evaluate the quality of their trend information and trend execution through sales results.

2.30
Trendstop delivers up-to-date catwalk colour and material information from the latest seasons.

2.31
Trendstop uses strong visuals to get the colour story across to audiences effectively.

2.32
Trendstop communication is directional and fashion forward.

What are the biggest menswear mega directions in the coming years? It is clear that menswear is changing in the twenty-first century, offering much more excitement and possibilities. My menswear forecast for the twenty-first century is that menswear will experience the same emancipation as womenswear did in the twentieth century. The last century for women began with corsets, bonnets and long skirts and ended with a woman being able to wear almost anything she wants, for almost any occasion. Today, there are still many taboos in menswear, particularly in business and workwear. By the end of the century there will be a lot more freedom and unisex comfort introduced into menswear, but in a way that is still masculine. For example, in Arabic cultures men wear long garments that are reminiscent of dresses. We are seeing this movement already infiltrating more forward menswear categories through elongated T-shirts, sweatshirts and knits. I predict that by the end of this century, a man will wear a similarly varied unisex wardrobe as today's contemporary woman and feel perfectly masculine. Mentally and in his daily life he will feel freer, more family oriented and less governed by a 9-to-5 job, in the same way women have gained freedom in society in the past 100 years, both at home and at work.

BLUER THAN BLUE

Blue evolves with an almost luminous quality, landing between cobalt and sapphire.

2.31

APRICOT CAMEL

Camel brown is upgraded to Fashion Colour status with a hint of peachy apricot, infusing the classic neutral with added warmth.

2.32

CHAPTER SUMMARY

This chapter has explored how trend develops into fashion and how fashion ultimately becomes clothing. The chapter also introduced trend structure theory, explaining how a trend can be broken down into trend units from larger structures. A lifestyle trend, for example, consists not only of fashion trends but also other trends that relate to culture and how we live.

The central theme of the chapter was trend thinking and how this can be incorporated into menswear design thinking. We introduced important theoretical approaches, such as diffusion of innovation, meme theory and tipping point theory. Trend thinking helps trend professionals consider society and culture and not just end products. Collections and accessories (i.e., the products) are the end result of the design cycle, but as a trend professional you need to understand the 'before' and 'after' as well. In addition to the theoretical models that exist, this chapter also discussed the intuitive approach: what intuition is and how one can learn to trust it.

We discussed the main trend concepts of mega, macro and micro trends along with the importance of understanding fashion change and the cycle of trends to see how often, and in what form, styles return. The complexities of trend timelines and the need for a trend professional to work simultaneously with several timelines at once were also clarified. You may find yourself simultaneously doing next season's analysis, preparing a forecast for three seasons ahead, and analyzing the past season's retail for yet another report. Because of the overlap of seasons and the spiralling nature of trends, a trend professional must be able to multitask and cultivate good project and time management skills.

HOMEWORK ASSIGNMENTS

1. Look at the past ten seasons of menswear catwalk coverage to analyse the silhouettes, such as the trouser length and width, to see if there are some noticeable changes.
2. Go to an area or café in your city where early adopters go and survey the men. See if you can spot any fads and analyse whether they will stay fads or become bigger trends. Explain your reasons.
3. Choose five trends in menswear today and identify the drivers for those trends.
4. List five mega, macro and micro trends and analyse the connections among them.
5. Look at recent menswear catwalk coverage and see what micro trends you can pull from the shows.

DISCUSSION ACTIVITIES AND PROJECTS

1. Identify fads that are not limited to fashion (think of social media, language etc.). Which do you think will evolve into bigger trends?
2. List the memes you are composed of and explore which ones you have adopted via vertical or horizontal flow.
3. Are there groups of people that do not belong to any of the consumer categories identified in the diffusion of innovation theories?
4. Can you identify mega trends that will impact the way we live?

KEY WORDS

cyclical	mega
fad	meme
fashion change	micro
macro	trend timeline

3.1

3.1
Retail is one of the
biggest sectors of
fashion that uses
trend information.

3

Menswear Retail and Trends

LEARNING OBJECTIVES

- Explore menswear trends in the larger context of retail.
- Apply trend data to menswear retail.
- Understand the importance of trends and merchandising.
- Differentiate between categories of menswear retail.
- Define various types of retail venues.
- Examine how brands can use trends to be more competitive.
- Research the menswear market as a whole.

INTRODUCTION

Retail – referring to the broader concept of the commercial activity of selling and buying – is one of the largest sectors to use trend services. Trend data and information can be used in numerous ways and in various sectors of menswear retail. For example, it can be used in the design of the actual product, if the retailer has its own brand, or it can be used in buying as an investment guide for the next season. Merchandisers work closely with buyers and with designers in order to make sure the product is sellable and on trend. In addition, visual merchandising has to make the windows and retail floor interesting and attractive: tired and old retail environments do not inspire customers to part with their cash. Trend work allows brands to be able to target customers with the right product at the right time, in order to maximize profit.

Menswear retail can be broken down into fast, mid, premium and high-end (luxury) fashion. In addition, there are made-to-measure and other retail services, such as customization and online re-sell platforms. Each of these sectors can be affected by the changing moods of the buyer, which is why it is vital to have an in-depth understanding of customer demographics and psychographics.

Fast fashion retail is closely associated with catwalks, so catwalk analysis is essential. The fast fashion trend consumer is not an early adopter, but is somewhere in early to late majority in the customer adaptation curve (see Chapter 2). Mid-level and premium retail are more established and put a lot of focus on mechanizing, basing purchase decisions on statistical data, which places them firmly in the late majority category. High-end menswear brands are often considered trend setters, yet they also follow closely what the competition is doing. All these areas combined create a dynamic menswear retail market that is worth over 440 billion dollars globally (Business Wire 2015).

Brands are a big part of the retail concept and must utilize trend information effectively. Trends based on culture and society, especially those used in long term strategies, can set a firm foundation for a brand. Trends that have a significant influence in today's retail are e-commerce – how electronic media is quickly adapting to people's needs and desires – and the significance of celebrity as a driving force for sales.

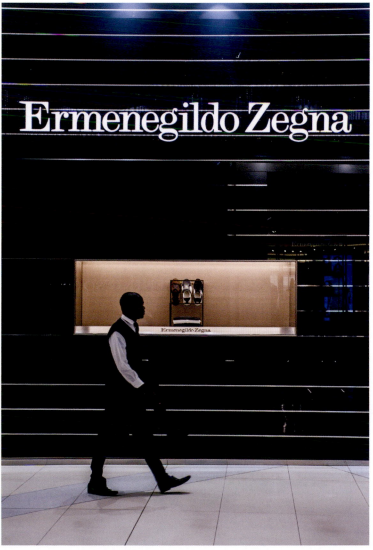

3.2

MENSWEAR RETAIL VENUES

Retail is the sale of goods or services to a consumer. The three main menswear categories are independent fashion retailers, multiple retailers and department stores. However, brands have also explored new concepts in retail – for example, pop-up shops and lifestyle stores. All of these outlets amalgamate the full consumer experience, not only the tangible product. In addition to brick and mortar stores, e-commerce plays a significant role for retailers.

It is important to understand the behaviour of both the retailer and the consumer. Most retailers offer timeless classics and basic lines that are best sellers season after season, which will be updated with trend-driven product. Knowledge of trends is essential to staying competitive and understanding what men need. It is vital to monitor products in the agenda-setting menswear retail environment the world over.

MONO-BRAND RETAIL

Mono-brand retail offers the customer a total brand experience, from apparel and accessories to brand extensions such as watches and perfumes. Mono-brand retail is usually led by a 'flagship' store that represents the brand values in total. This type of retail environment is interesting to see from a visual merchandising point of view. Observe the retail architecture and the use of light and colour in display of items. These can provide clues to how retailers are enticing customers to spend money. Trend services are invaluable to brands as this provides them with an outside entity evaluating their brand direction.

3.3
Companies such as Burberry are examples of mono-brand retailers offering the customer a total brand experience.

3.3

INDEPENDENTS

Independents are retailers that have a small retail presence that are not owned by a larger company. Usually independents occupy a single space, although some do have multiple locations. Independent retailers, such as Matches in London and Maxfield in Los Angeles, will cater to a core client that favours the brand environment they offer.

Directional retailers are a type of independent retailer, such as OAK, New York and LN:CC, London; they cater to the early adaptor. This category is interesting for the trend analyst as it provides carefully curated collections and brands that are not necessarily seen in other markets.

3.4

3.4
London independent Diverso specializes in Made in Italy clothes.

3.5

MULTIPLES/CHAINS

Multiples, or chains, are retailers that have several close-to-identical retail channels. They are mainly mono-brand stores, such as Hackett or Superdry, and are often international but managed from a central office. As in any retail, there are chains that cater to every level of customer. For example, Zara stores have the exact same window and floor merchandising policies, no matter the location, which makes them globally uniform. Yet other mono-brand chains, such as Camper, work carefully to make sure that their stores are each slightly different, taking into consideration local architecture and culture. Although Camper is a chain, each store feels like an independent boutique.

DEPARTMENT STORES

Department stores, with their multitude of products and brands, make an ideal place to observe the latest in retail management and brand communication. These are the spaces where brands fight for the shopper's attention, making presentation and communication the focal point. The trend interest areas in department stores are the directional brand areas. These areas are good places to explore not only which brands and new styles the retailer has chosen to sell, but also what type of customer shops there. Department stores such as Liberty of London or Barney's New York want to have their buying on the trend pulse, offering brands that are up and coming and desirable.

3.5
Hackett is a mono-brand chain that has a growing number of stores across the globe.

CONCEPT/LIFESTYLE STORES

Concept or lifestyle stores are multi-brand stores with a curated experience aimed at a particular group of consumers. These carry not only apparel, but also other products, such as books, music and even food that the target type of consumer might buy. These retail environments are independent, but can also be found as concessions within department stores, with a heavy focus on the design of the retail environment. Here you may find directional labels and items. This type of retail caters to the early adopter, often considered the trend-setting sector of retail. The lifestyle stores usually buy into the latest gadgets and brands that may be of interest to the early consumer, providing a perfect platform for trends to evolve.

CREATIVE RETAIL

Pop-up stores (sometimes referred to as 'guerrilla' shops) are examples of creative retail and are employed by retailers as new ways to entice customers to spend their money. Pop-up stores are temporary shops that occupy unused retail spaces or even other surprisingly unexpected spaces. Under the creative retail umbrella, it is possible to have various other new innovative retail venues. One recent example of how such retailing can prove successful is Boxpark in London, where the retail space seems permanent, but can be easily unassembled. These recycled shipping containers make for an interesting retail experience, with a hint of a sustainability stamp of approval.

3.6

3.6
The Liberty of London store carries a variety of directional menswear brands alongside more classic brands.

3.7

E-COMMERCE

Online clothes shopping is still the fastest growing area of retail. Companies are trying hard to lure more and more people into buying from online shops, rather than the more expensive brick-and-mortar option. Ultimately companies want to reach omnichannel uniformity, where the product is delivered in an equal manner, regardless of where and how it is purchased. This means, for example, that if a product is on sale in the brick-and-mortar store, it would also be on sale in all the other channels the brand uses at the same time. With multichannel thinking, various channels are used to help

with the decision making (e.g., laptops, smart phones and retail spaces). Omnichannel offers consumers a seamless retail experience, whether they are physically in the retail space or not, using their devices to help with decision making. This type of omni/multichannel marketing is being used by brands more often, as it presents huge potential benefits.

Companies such as Burberry are taking full advantage of digital opportunities, offering the ability to buy straight off their catwalk via the Internet (right after the collections are shown) as well as from the brick-and-mortar shops.

3.7
Boxpark London is an example of creative retail, where brands can reach a new consumer without a huge brick-and-mortar investment.

3.8

3.9

3.8
Mr. Porter is the most successful menswear online retailer. E-tailers such as Mr. Porter sell well-curated and bankable looks that are often similar to their trend pages.

3.9
Burberry takes online shopping to another level. Collections can be bought straight off the catwalk show either online or at the store.

MENSWEAR RETAIL CONSUMER

In order to better understand retail, we need to analyse the retail consumer and their behaviour. It is important to analyse the demographics (for example age, race and sex) and the psychographics (for example, attitudes and interests) of the targeted customer group. Generally it is understood that demographics is about the 'who' and psychographics about the 'why'. Whereas demographics can be measured statistically, psychographic research is more difficult to present as simple data and therefore requires deeper research and understanding in order to understand how internal states affect how men spend. Comparing men's attitudes, interests and opinions can bring more insight and understanding to behaviour regarding menswear.

MENSWEAR DEMOGRAPHY

Demography is the statistical study of people that relates to a group's education, nationality, religion or ethnicity. For example, ageing and migration would be a category of demographic study. Demographic studies rely largely on quantitative data and focus on the target customer. For example, statistics on the ethnic component of cities or neighbourhoods may help to determine the languages spoken, or what might be on offer at the retail level in those particular neighbourhoods.

Trend prediction and analysis has recently taken great interest in ageing and how that demographic information can impact future purchasing. According to a report from A. T. Kearney and The Consumer Goods Forum (2013), the population over 60 years of age is the fastest growing consumer demographic globally. What does this mean for the future of lifestyle and fashion? Will older men also spend money on apparel and fashion? If so, what type? These are some of the bigger questions that demographic trend field study may help you to understand. For retail, demographic trends are useful for long-term planning to gain a better understanding of the direction men, as a group and in subgroups, are heading in.

3.10

MENSWEAR PSYCHOGRAPHICS

Psychographics is the study of personality and focuses on interests, attitudes and opinions, also known as the IAO variable. Other behavioural variables, such as sexual preferences and morals, can be studied in order to get a more accurate target for retail marketing activity. Psychographics are helpful for retail to gain a good understanding of their target customer. The information is gathered from surveys and various census services. There are professional companies that conduct psychographics research for larger companies.

Psychographics research is valuable as it relates to the culture of fashion and dress. Attitudes, interests and opinions influence what men are wearing at the moment, and any changes will reflect on the future of menswear as well. Trying to decipher why men buy is an important part of trend research, especially analysis and prediction. Monitoring men's IAO variable will help you to see if there are patterns and to notice how changes in dress and taste for fashion relate to the way men live.

One recent big trend is men taking more interest in various traditional craft activities, such as cooking, patronizing traditional barbershops, DIY (do it yourself) and making things in general. This, in turn, has influenced menswear, which now offers more utilitarian items, such as raw denim, plaid shirts, canvas outerwear and even aprons. In this instance, the early adopter interest has directly influenced the dress of this group.

It is good practice to back up your research with psychographic data. As mentioned in previous chapters, data supporting the general trend vision is something that companies and clients like to see; it adds great value and insight to your presentation.

3.11

3.10
Older consumer groups are the fastest growing demographic. Nick Wooster, a style icon for the young and the old, influences all age groups.

3.11
Psychographics is the study of personality, focusing on interests, attitudes and opinions of people. Psychographics are helpful for retail to gain a good understanding of the target customer.

MENSWEAR RETAIL CATEGORIES

Retail caters to various categories of consumers, with some crossover. The main categories are fast, mid, premium and luxury fashion. These are usually based on the price of the product (determined by the quality of materials, production costs etc.). Each one of these retail categories uses trend information in one way or another.

FAST FASHION

One of the greatest catalytic movements of recent decades in retail has been the birth of fast fashion, which has singlehandedly changed the face of fashion retail. Fast fashion is the production of collections within incredibly fast turnaround times. Fast fashion often gets 'inspiration' from catwalks and is able to quickly produce and present the product to the retail market long before the catwalk designers themselves have produced the original garment. However, this is changing, as some high-end brands are now preparing collections to be ready right at the catwalk show.

Fashion catwalks were previously only for buyers and select press. Now they are a public spectacle, with a diverse range of people wanting to be part of them. Fast fashion companies base their retail philosophies on the consumers' impatience. It is possible to see all the catwalks' glamour today and buy into it just a few weeks later. Fast fashion has also contributed to the democracy of fashion, in that it has made catwalk fashions financially accessible to a much larger – often, though not limited to – younger market. Fast fashion has also gained popularity; celebrities wear brands such as Primark and, in so doing, they give fast fashion the credibility it needed.

Fast fashion is prone to the ever-changing tastes of the consumer. Companies such as Zara and H&M must be timely and accurate in selecting which trend products to develop. Because there is so much inspirational seasonal information, it is hard for fast fashion companies to come to a logical creative conclusion about which elements to include in their products; therefore, slight variations are required. Companies such as Zara, Primark, H&M and Forever 21 have in-house design offices. They can produce collections that are completely catwalk and street trend driven, catering to the majority of customer categories. Fast fashion is the largest retail sector that uses catwalk, trade show and street-style reporting to help with design and buying direction.

3.12

MID-LEVEL RETAIL

Mid-level fashion retail tends to be aimed at an older demographic than that of fast fashion and offers basics that are updated seasonally. Mid-level retail shops such as Gap and Banana Republic have some seasonal trend items, but rely heavily on the mass market with their basic items. Mid-level menswear is seasonal and follows the classic delivery of apparel (i.e., spring/summer and autumn/winter). Many mid-level menswear retailers are international chains. Some mid-level retailers even offer higher level product to attract new customers. Usually if a retailer is known for one level of product, it is difficult to change the customer's pre-conceived notions of quality/price – especially when attempting to change from mid to higher level categories.

Mid-level retail design and buying teams will find trend information beneficial because they are positioned between the young, fast fashion consumer and the more mature, premium consumer. Trend information will help them position themselves better. There are many inspirational trend stories that work well with the mid-level market, from visual merchandising to colour selection of collections. The mid-level market uses trends to create a bankable buying strategy, often created in-house with the merchandising team. The trend direction can come from trend agencies or from in-house study of catwalk and street trends.

3.12
Fast fashion companies such as Primark have in-house designers who monitor various sources of trends.

PREMIUM

Premium menswear retail is very aware of early adopter consumer habits. Premium labels such as Hugo Boss and Calvin Klein closely monitor the latest directions in trends. In premium retail, the timing of the trend delivery is very important. A trend cannot be introduced to the retail audience too early – but often it needs to be just a little earlier than mid-level retailers. Premium wants to appear to be delivering something new to the consumer, while not scaring them away. It sells trend-driven product alongside seasonally updated best sellers. Premium retail uses trend information most often in the design or buying, closely following the data from the merchandising department.

LUXURY

Luxury retail, whether a brand or a department store, is often regarded as timeless and not necessarily tied into the trends market. Luxury is also hard to define today, since it can mean so many things to different people. In menswear, brands such as Prada and department stores such as Neiman Marcus are regarded as leaders and trend setters at the luxury level of menswear. However, they too follow trends and conduct careful consumer behaviour research in order to make certain that their products are commercially desirable.

3.13
Hugo Boss is an example of premium level retail. They often have a strong brand DNA, yet closely follow contemporary directions to stay competitive.

3.14
Neiman Marcus is a luxury-level department store with multiple stores across the USA. They sell staple menswear, such as Prada and Gucci, with the occasional update of lesser known names, such as Juun.J.

3.15
Savile Row is outside the normal influence of trends but still reacts to today's needs.

3.13

MADE TO MEASURE AND BESPOKE

'Made to measure' occurs when a pair of shoes or clothing is made for your standard measurements; 'bespoke' is made exactly to fit you from high quality materials selected by you and your maker in a true personalized service. Bespoke is not really a menswear fashion category as such, but it is still trend-prone at some level. Take, for example, Savile Row, where styles suggested for clients appeal to a contemporary man. The styles might be classic, but they are not outdated or historic.

Any trend, such as the width of the trouser leg or the width of the shoulder, has slowly been adapted to today's standards. The younger generation of tailors is especially influenced by what men wear, not necessarily on catwalks, but in a combination of peer and street styles. One element of made to measure and bespoke that is clearly driven by trends is the fabric selection that comes from the mills to the tailors.

3.14

3.15

BUYING, MERCHANDISING AND VISUAL MERCHANDISING

Within retail strategy, the buying, merchandising and visual merchandising departments work together closely in order to create the best possible environment for the consumer. All these departments can benefit greatly by understanding how trends work and how they help the retailer find a well-balanced retail mix. A buyer can use trend information, mainly close-to-season analysis, to help with the buying decisions. Merchandisers will compare the numeric data to project what will sell and be desirable in the future. Visual merchandisers take the material and create forms of visual communication that will entice shoppers to part with their money. Visual merchandisers can also find trend information useful by creating windows and retail floors that communicate the sign of the times.

BUYING

Buying and trends are closely connected. Some buyers use trend agency services to get inspiration for next season's purchases. They can simply view the material to get a full understanding of what the signals are for the new season. Other buying offices make their own buying guides based on agency information, combined with gathered trend intelligence. Buyers for exclusive retailers such as Liberty of London or Jeffrey NYC have to consider buying bankable trend items, avoiding exactly the same products as the competition. The buying selection process overall differs greatly depending on the level, the country and the type of retailer that is in question.

MERCHANDISING

The role of the merchandiser is to create the right product mix for retail. The merchandiser will look at the historical sales data and compare it with current buying in order to create a confident retail sales projection. The projection should not be based exclusively on numbers and spreadsheets, which is why it is important for merchandisers to look into trend data as well. Merchandising works closely with the buyer as well as designers in order to create a well-balanced product environment that appeals to consumers. Trend information will help merchandisers to make educated guesses as to what will sell by looking at close-to-retail trend reporting and by following the general lifestyles and needs of that particular brand target group.

VISUAL MERCHANDISING

The main purpose of visual merchandising is to attract clients into the retail space and to make them stay until a purchase is made. There are various systems and studied methods to do this. Trends are a very useful tool for this purpose; people like to be in inspiring spaces.

The windows are there to seduce the consumer into the fantasy world of the brand. Often windows have eye-catching products that are bought in small numbers, for the sole purpose of attracting attention, or windows and in-store merchandising can simply tell the customer what is available and recommended in the store. Visual merchandisers stay on top of of trends in fashion, as well as trends in their specific field.

3.16

3.16
Barneys NY is famous for its elaborate windows.

3.17

MICHAEL FISHER
Creative Director – Menswear, Fashion Snoops

Michael Fisher oversees the creation of trend forecasting and analysis for the men's market at Fashion Snoops (FS), as well as lending a hand in the management of the active, kids, young men's, grooming and denim sections. In addition, he spends a large portion of his time with the agency's co-founder and chief creative officer on a multitude of consulting projects with big-name clients that range from sneaker retailers and automobile makers to toy manufacturers and chemical companies. Finally, as one of Fashion Snoops' creative directors, he gets a lot of face-to-face time with the sales and marketing divisions on how to sell the site, coming up with new products and content, while going to client appointments to present trends. Michael also works closely with the art director and graphic design team on the overall aesthetic of their site and services and how to evolve them in keeping with new graphic trends.

What is the Fashion Snoops approach to trends? Fashion Snoops approaches trends as a living, breathing organic entity that changes and evolves from the first point of forecast (approximately twenty-four months ahead of time), all the way to when the product actually hits the selling floor. Culture is the foundation of our company and the cornerstone of everything we do. Nothing just exists out of nowhere. Our entire global team is constantly digging into our personal and collective Zeitgeists for what is emerging in culture (lifestyle and consumer trends, travel and leisure, retail merchandising and presentation, technology, among other elements). We put a lot of effort into our culture section and make sure that every single thing we do comes from a cultural macro trend first. We then track the shifts as the world happens around us, a major piece of gold for our many clients. Fashion is just a secondary part of that, and of course, everything that happens on the runways and later at retail is first born in a cultural movement. That is what makes us different from others who call out a handful of trends two years in advance and place them in a metaphorical drawer, never to be heard from again. We know trends will change constantly, and we stick with them.

How did you end up working with trends? My entire life, I wanted to be a broadcast journalist, appearing on TV and reporting the world news. Once I got to college, I took a course on trend forecasting with my university's Department of Fashion and fell in love overnight. It awoke all of these skills of foresight and analysis in me that I never knew I had. My professor (who had just come from a forecasting job at Cotton Inc.) encouraged me to change my major, and I did. I never looked back, and it's been fourteen years in the industry at this point. Every single day is different, and I love it. I worked on the retail side of the industry for approximately six years (at Ralph Lauren in advertising and marketing, at Barneys

3.17
Michael Fisher, Creative Director – Menswear, Fashion Snoops

New York as a men's designer buyer, and finally, Bloomingdale's as a men's fashion director), and each gig I got, I made sure it involved trend forecasting in a larger way. Then in 2008, I transitioned over to Stylesight (now merged with WGSN) and built their men's section from pretty much scratch. After nearly four years, I went over to Fashion Snoops to lead the men's team, and I've been here for four years.

What is your view on menswear at the moment? It is a truly exciting time to be in menswear. It is the only segment of the industry to have grown on a year-to-year basis since the recession of 2008. The speed of trends is picking up velocity every single year, and more than anything, I am so impressed with menswear consumers and how educated they are about personal style and the industry as a whole. Niche men's media has never been better, especially the online world (Hypebeast, Highsnobiety, Valet Mag etc.). I think currently the evolving fashion calendar is certainly affecting menswear as more designers are wanting to show men's and women's collections at the same time. This season, many of our favourite, most influential brands have dropped out of men's fashion weeks in London, Milan and New York, and that worries me a bit. I don't want to see any of the momentum we've built in the last five years going away. Men overall are evolving as fast as the world. It's no longer unacceptable to care about your personal style (both clothing and accessories, as well as grooming). They demand trend-right merchandise that tells a story, and I love that.

Do you have a specific methodology or approach to explore trends? My personal methodology is to just be an active citizen of the world. I am hungry for every bit of culture I can get, and I make sure to not just stay within the confines of menswear on a day-to-day basis. I absorb every bit of media I can get my hands

3.18
Fashion Snoops S/S 17 Key Items trends story.

3.18

3.19

on, including social media, and truly have a FOMO (fear of missing out) approach at my job. I constantly take in every bit of noise that passes me by, even random walks down a block in midtown Manhattan, and then think, 'What does that mean?' I try and not get too involved in what others are doing. My most important skill is the ability to tell new and interesting stories for my clients – to show them how exciting menswear can truly be.

What is the most important part for trend research for you? I think the most important part of my research probably comes from museum exhibitions, influential artists and emerging runway collections. The street isn't as important as it used to be, since so many people are trying to fit in a certain mold, a mold often already set by my team in the months prior. It's not as authentic, let's say. I am looking to who is creating the most buzz out there and how can that translate to a story for the men's market.

How much do you rely on data on your research, or are you more intuition-driven? I would say some data is important, but my gut instinct is what really guides me. I take note of everything, including every time I walk into a store, noticing what is the big-picture message and even what is NOT selling (often, that is more telling than anything). I look at some industry numbers about what is up-trending and what isn't performing at retail, but my instinct is why I'm good at this job, so I don't every underestimate the power of myself. We also gather our own internal research from a global team of researchers and correspondents who are our eyes and ears all over the world.

3.19
Fashion Snoops Mood story Nearshore for SS 2017.

3.20
Raw coast colour/ elements story for S/S2017 from Fashion Snoops.

3.20

What areas of fashion industry can benefit your information? We have a wide range of clients, ranging from mass retailers and luxury department stores to chemical companies, global active brands and consumer goods corporations. Everyone can benefit from knowing how consumers' wants will change in the coming years, as well as knowing the major cultural shifts in store for our world. Not everyone has the ability or the time to this kind of research and analysis, so we do it for them. We like to consider ourselves an extended part of our clients' teams.

What is the role of customer behaviour in your strategy? As I mentioned, it all starts with culture. We hold consumer behaviour under a constant microscope and it will certainly affect every single thing we forecast. We want to know what drives them into new behaviours or what holds them back. As I said, as much as newness and innovation drive us, we also need to know why they will NOT do something. They are equally as important.

Fashion system is going through some changes at the moment. How do you think this will affect your work? I think that due to what is called 'fast fashion fatigue,' luxury brands and designers got tired of their work being knocked off in a matter of weeks. Six months later, consumers are mostly over what these brands worked so hard to create. So, they're revamping how their work is presented and this includes dropping out of the typical fashion calendar. For us as forecasters, it just means we'll have less visual confirmation leading up to when the merchandise actually hits the stores. We'll have our own private glimpses by going to showrooms and talking to other editors, but mostly, we'll need to even further trust our instinct about what's coming down the line. In many ways, it's taking us back to the time when information wasn't as accessible to the general public.

What do you think will be key menswear directions in the coming season? For fall/winter 2017/18, we are forecasting a major shift in individual style. From a heavy emphasis on 70s-inspired texture and overstated silhouettes to a visually stunning merging of old Hollywood Art Deco to super contemporary, museum-quality minimalism, it will be a season all about unique touches. In addition to cultural macro trends like new luxury and what we call 'nowstalgia,' we're also tracking the importance of modern revolutions and standing up for a cause. The alienation felt in politics currently is truly affecting collections for next fall, including the concept of 'positive propaganda', soft utility and a regal approach at archetypes of men's uniforms through the ages.

3.21

EMBER TODD
Colour and Trend Manager for Chaco Brand at Wolverine Worldwide

Ember Todd is based in Grand Rapids, Michigan. Her role is to seasonally identify consumer trends, colour palettes and key colourways so Chaco can design the right product at the right time for its consumer.

How did you end up working with trends? In one of my past positions as a footwear colour designer, I was a part of an in-depth project employing methods of social science to study our brand's consumer behaviour. That opportunity absolutely shaped my view of how to identify deep and continuing trends that truly resonate with people on an emotional level. I have honed my methods over the years, but this is still the very genesis of my process. When the opportunity came my way to work on consumer trend forecasting for Chaco, a brand with a small but fiercely loyal consumer following, I jumped at it.

What does a trend-forecasting department do? Trend forecasting has such a diverse definition from one industry to the next. To me, trend forecasting is most valuable when it identifies influences and directions of the consumer mindset over a long period of time. So instead of identifying the 'tiny home' movement as a trend, we identify the underlying influence or emotion that drives that action – the desire for personal and financial freedom. This enables us to pinpoint shifts in the needs and desires of the marketplace and innovate products and solutions to meet those future needs. People often identify the colour and trend role as a final finishing of the product, but true trend direction identifies where to position your product and in which market. We observe, analyse and distil an extreme amount of information to help point our brand in the right direction for the future.

What is your view on menswear at the moment? Menswear is fascinating right now. Men's specific fashion is definitely gaining momentum with the addition of New York Fashion Week: Men's, the growth of menswear fashion flagship stores, the rise of male supermodels and men being the fastest growing demographic on Pinterest. If you're not focusing on menswear trends in your business right now, you will miss out.

Do you have a specific methodology or approach to explore trends? Each season I do my best to immerse myself in research – observation of related industries, relevant articles from as many sources as possible, trend forecasting from industry-leading sources, new books – anything and everything to get as large of a sampling of information as possible. When I go into research mode it's really about letting the information speak to me more than proving a certain idea I may have. Once I have read and reread everything, I note reoccurring themes or patterns. This allows me to group the patterns by bigger themes or connecting

3.21
Ember Todd, the Colour and Trend Manager for Chaco Brand at Wolverine Worldwide.

ideas and create the key trend insights. From there it's about adding inspirational imagery that feels true to the theme and gives a consistent style direction for the trend. Having the initial depth of research helps me to put weight behind the trends and ultimately builds confidence with our brand team and sales force. My goal is always to find the 'why' – the underlying behaviour that is driving the action so we can design towards the physical or emotional needs of our consumer.

How is the trend information used? We use the trends to help identify the needs of our consumer, whether in key silhouettes, multi-function uses, technical features, design cues, materialization, colouration, novel production methods, marketing or sales initiatives, or photo shoot styling.

How does merchandising benefit from trends? Do the trends filter to communication? Our trends certainly help to shape our merchandising. After the trends are built we place each upcoming footwear style into one of our corresponding trends. Linking each style to a trend helps them to have specific direction and purpose for existing within our line. We even use the trends to help merchandise our line by colour. Each trend has a unique aesthetic colour-wise, which helps us design and develop a dynamic seasonal range.

Trends do filter to our communication. Consumers often are reacting to what is going on in the world, such as politics, economic troubles or booms, the environment, wars, social change – all weighty subjects that affect behaviour in curious ways. The way to communicate with people has everything to do with the current social climate and what the consumer really needs emotionally at that time. Trends identify those needs so you can speak to the consumers in a consistent and appropriate voice across all advertising and social platforms.

3.22
'We observe, analyse, and distill an extreme amount of information to help point our brand in the right direction for the future'. Ember Todd, Chaco.

3.22

What is the role of consumer behaviour in your strategy? Each season we review the most recent year's sales to glean insights into what our consumer gravitated to. It has helped us to better understand buying behaviour, especially when it comes to product colour. We are able to put weight behind our seasonal colouration and merchandising by analyzing retail numbers and applying similar logic to our designs as we develop the future line.

What do you think will be key menswear directions in the coming season? With the turmoil in our social climate and the prevailing lack of consumer confidence after the Great Recession, I see a continuation of heritage silhouettes, classic and quality materials and throwback design collaborations. People continue to look backwards to 'better times', which is why timeless designs are currently resonating so well with consumers. One of my favourite shows from the FW16 NYFWM was Joseph Abboud. The line felt timeless but modern, contrasting but coordinated, familiar but fresh. It took a meaningful step away from all of the overtly casual athleisure lines and brought some life and style back into menswear dress.

Are there any big trends you see influencing footwear companies in the next decade or so? One of the biggest trends we've been tracking is the shift in consumer dollars from buying products to buying memorable experiences. People are continuing to buy less so they can do more, which means each of the few items they purchase must do double duty when it comes to usage. There is also an expectation of quality and durability as people turn from the fast fashion trend of recent years. Today's footwear needs to perform when needed, such as hiking, running or travel, but also must work in the context of everyday, casual situations. This helps explain the continuing rise of classic styles. When consumers buy fewer items for multiple usage occasions with an extended lifespan, they want those pieces to be classic and enduring styles.

3.23
Chaco uses information from various sources to decide on colour, material and mood direction.

3.23

CHAPTER SUMMARY

In this chapter we have explored the world of menswear retail. We first defined the main venues of retail: mono-brand and multi-brand stores, including independents, multiple (chains), department stores and concept/lifestyle stores. We also discussed experimental retail venues and the increasing importance of e-commerce. Each of these venues values the demographic and psychographic information that trend work can apply to its consumer.

We distinguished the role of trend forecasting in the retail worlds of fast fashion, mid-level, premium, luxury and bespoke. We finally looked at other areas of menswear retail that uses trend data, including merchandising, buying and visual merchandising. Trends are a vital part of the everyday menswear retail business, where companies are doing their best to provide a product that consumers want and that is profitable.

HOMEWORK ASSIGNMENTS

1. Create a questionnaire that could be used to conduct a psychographic IAO (Interest, Attitudes, Opinions) study.
2. Select a brand and research which areas of the brand could be updated using trend information.
3. Report and analyse trends from city window merchandising.

DISCUSSION ACTIVITIES AND PROJECTS

1. Discuss in class the different types of retail you have in your city or area.
2. Discuss the differences between psychographics and demography.
3. List various ways retail can benefit from trends analysis.

KEY WORDS

demography
flagship
IAO
independents
mono-brand
multi-brand
multichannel
omnichannel
psychographics

4.1

4.1
A systematic show
analysis will provide
a solid foundation
for close-to-season
trends.

4

Trend Details for Business

LEARNING OBJECTIVES

- Analyse catwalks, including student catwalks.
- Gather information from street-style coverage.
- Evaluate information gathered from retail.
- Compare short-term and long-term analysis.
- Select the required information for near-season use.

INTRODUCTION

In this chapter we will explore what information should be gathered from catwalks, street styling and trade shows. These three areas form the basis for a well-rounded trend analysis, which can serve as a starting point for a longer-term trend forecast. Catwalks are usually considered near-season analysis, which is used by companies that want to understand the current state of the menswear business.

Most catwalk information and presentations are available online almost instantly, which is invaluable. However, because this information is accessible to everyone, it is important for the analyst to use his or her skills to provide a more detailed analysis of the catwalk. Catwalks can also offer long-term vision and material for analysis. Brands such as J. W. Anderson, Henrik Vibskov and Vetements are often too early for mainstream retail, yet may shape the future by entering the marketplace though early retail. Mainstream retail, such as department store brands, will most likely look at catwalks from less experimental designers rather than the boundary-pushing brands mentioned above: in the end, a good retailer knows from experience what its consumers will buy into.

Street style is considered short-term trend information simply because the men photographed mainly wear items that are available to buy already. Trade show information gathering takes place about six months before items go to retail, making it a good starting point for longer-term trend forecasting. In addition, student catwalks, which are less commercial, will add an edge to catwalk analysis with their often more experimental designs. Wherever the fashion product is presented, whether runway or retail, there is a wealth of trend information to be gathered. Companies also use trend analysis to study the competition, to both stay inline with the competition and also to stay a step ahead of them.

INNOVATORS, INTERPRETERS AND IMITATORS

Catwalk, street-style and trade show information is useful for various levels of the menswear business. Retailers and brands can be broken down into innovators, interpreters and imitators. An innovator would be a fashion brand that presents something new to the system, while interpreters look to the innovators for inspiration in order to develop collections, and imitators simply copy (mainly the interpreters). Premium menswear retailers and brands (interpreters) are inspired by early trend analysis. Mainstream and fast fashion companies will focus more on close-to-season, late trend analysis. They use information (catwalks, etc.) to 'imitate' the premium brands. Experimental brands are aware of what is happening in the fashion scene; they are usually the ones bringing something new to the fashion world.

CATWALK ANALYSIS

Catwalks are one of the main sources of trend information for many companies, especially for mainstream brands (for example, mid-level retailers such as Macy's) and media. Catwalks take place twice a year; in June for the following spring/summer season and in January for the following autumn/winter season. Most companies follow these classic fashion seasons; however, some, such as Vetements, Tom Ford and Burberry, have started to challenge the seasonal systems. In the case of Burberry and Tom Ford, it could be that the decision to challenge the seasonal systems has been done in order to be able to offer something that is immediately available after the shows. With Vetements, the new model is to simplify the buying system with earlier timings. The main reason for companies to find new ways to promote collections is to maximize profits. It remains to be seen if the rest of the fashion system will follow suit and what the prevailing system will be.

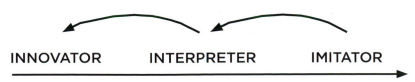

INNOVATOR   INTERPRETER   IMITATOR

4.2

4.2
The fashion idea's journey starts with Innovation, which inspires the Interpreter, who in turn is copied by the Imitator.

The advent of the Internet has meant that it is very easy to view a collection after the shows and most online fashion magazines have images that can be viewed almost immediately. One of the biggest trend consumers are fast fashion companies that will look at the collections and quickly copy them for mass consumption. This is often viewed negatively, yet fast fashion is the most consumed sector of fashion and catwalks are increasingly influencing trends and mass consumption though replication.

The main areas to study when analyzing the catwalk are: mood, key looks, silhouette, surface and accessories.

Mood

The mood of the collection is often based on a theme set either by the creative director or the designer of the brand. This information is usually delivered in the beginning of the show in the form of a printed press release. This information is then communicated by fashion journalists, such as Tim Blanks, to a wider audience. When looking at the collection as a whole, it is often quite easy to see what the general theme is. The mood that is set by the designer can emerge from many different starting points of inspiration, which can be personal, subcultural or historical. Sometimes menswear collections are material driven. Designers such as Astrid Andersen will always have a strong brand DNA (luxury and sportswear, in her case) but will most likely have a thematic approach to collections as well.

When looking at the images from the shows, develop a vocabulary for mood. This also helps, as demonstrated later, with the organization of images. The mood can be defined by many descriptive words, such as 'somber', 'elegant', 'young', 'formal'. The theme of the collection, whether it is Victorian sailors or kung fu B-movies, should not be confused with the mood that it evokes. Mood is less specific and gives a general description of the collection, whereas the theme is about the inspirational source of the material.

4.3
Catwalks are not only about commercial, big-name brands. Trend setting design houses, such as Vetements, are the brands that can dictate what the early adopter will buy into.

4.4
Designers often have personal inspirational sources that are communicated to the international press. Here, an Astrid Andersen spring/summer 2016 collection inspired by a Singapore trip.

4.5
Big brands can have over 100 exits, as seen here in the Dolce & Gabbana show. Stylists will 'time' the collections strategically to entice the interest of the audience.

4.3

Key Looks

Key looks within a collection are either a styled combination of clothes that encapsulate the collection, or a key piece that does the same. The key looks may also reference different styles, whether they are office or holiday wear. Of course, the styling of the show and the way collections are presented also depends on the size of the collection. Dolce & Gabbana or Emporio Armani might have close to 100 exits, or runway looks, so the key-look strategy might differ. The average number of exits for menswear shows is somewhere around thirty, with smaller labels having even fewer.

Key looks can also be referred to by the press as 'must haves', or in the selling scene as 'best sellers'. Designers and stylists often have the strongest looks close the show. However, that may depend on the catwalk strategy, as they can also be used to open it.

4.4

4.5

4.6
The Balenciaga
spring/summer
2017 catwalk
combined a wider
top silhouette with
leg-hugging shorts
bottoms.

4.6

Silhouette

Menswear silhouettes often revolve around the slimness of the fit. Slim fit is associated with 'sharpness' and a 'clean' silhouette, especially in suits. These are all descriptive terms for the shape of clothes in relation to the body. Silhouette can also refer to the shoulders (padded or soft), the cut of suits and jackets and the length of trousers. The silhouette has changed quite a bit between decades, and although catwalks introduce new volumes all the time, adoption can be slow. The silhouette can be looser on top and tighter and more fitted in the bottom, as seen in Bottega Veneta and Saint Laurent spring/summer 2016 catwalks. The silhouette trend can naturally affect individual pieces as well, especially outerwear. Coats for men have been following the women's trend of being large and full of volume, as they were in the 1980s. The fit and silhouette are as trend prone as everything else in fashion. Look and compare some of the past seasons' silhouette changes, either in college fashion magazines or online. Give them descriptive names to build your trend vocabulary.

Surface

Surface refers to whatever fabric surface treatment is apparent in the catwalks. This can be print, graphics, colour and pattern, including the type of fabric used. Print and graphics are easy to spot on the catwalks and can provide good graphic content for a trend package. Patterns are also very trend prone, as seen with camouflage or florals. Popular patterns in recent seasons are Aztec motif prints and lumberjack plaids. Colour has been discussed throughout this book because it is such an important focus and often a main area of interest for designers and buyers alike. Colour is one of the main factors in purchasing decisions; hence, it is very important in a business sense. Colour often appears in catwalks a few seasons before it tips over into mainstream, so the catwalk is a great place to understand the future direction of colour trends, and retail is a perfect place to view mainstream colour direction.

CATWALK OBSERVATION

Have a look at some of the most recent catwalks from different cities in order to see if there is a common colour that appears in all of them. The colour does not necessarily have be to that of the full garment; it can also be a pop colour that appears on a smaller surface.

At the end of this chapter you'll see a colour exercise that will give you comprehensive experience on colour and the runway. Recently collections have been print and graphics heavy. However, has this peaked and is menswear going back to solid surfaces? Have a look at recent seasons to understand which are the must-have patterns for menswear today. Will they have lasting power?

4.7–4.8
Colour can also be categorized as part of the surface design and features in close-to-season catwalk reporting. In these two examples, look at how the same colour is used in a casual context versus a more formal one.

4.9
Accessories coverage has become important for trend consumers.

WASHED TEAL CASUAL
F/W 2016-17 CATWALK COLOUR FORECAST
trendstop

4.7

WASHED TEAL FORMAL
F/W 2016-17 CATWALK COLOUR FORECAST
trendstop

4.8

Accessories

Accessories are an important part of the fashion system because they are items that more people can afford (as opposed to main collection items). The key accessories are bags and shoes, but hats, eyewear, gloves, belts, scarves and even jewellery are all items closely followed and used in trend forecasting. Most online portals offer a details section providing close-ups of shoes and bags, and magazines such as *Show Details Men* and *Collezioni Uomo* offer lots of detail coverage on accessories.

Shoes are very closely monitored the moment catwalks are presented, and there are even blogs and special supplements focusing only on shoes. Recently, bags have also become very important items to watch on catwalks, simply because men have started to buy and wear more bags. One of the drivers of this trend is technology: the need to carry around tablets, laptops and associated peripherals.

One of the biggest new accessories of recent seasons is the hat. Fedoras and other felt hats for winter, and straw hats for summer, have seen a huge growth in use among men. This trend is partly celebrity driven (for example, Pharrell Willams) and partly the influence of street styling.

4.9

FILTERING THE CATWALK

It is essential to view all shows the moment they are available. There are many shows to see during each city's catwalk season, so although it isn't practical to view them all in detail immediately, it is advisable to at least scan through them the moment they are available. Analyse what you have seen after perusing all the shows from London, Milan, Paris and New York. The best way is to simply write down key moods and looks that initially emerge from the shows. Apps such as Vogue Runway are great tools to get a concise feed of looks into your device, helping with filtering.

Trend Tagging System

One system that works very well is building a keyword dictionary to help with both image categorizing and analyzing the collection. Using industry-standard vocabulary will help in writing reports that are understood by professionals. The tagging process involves tagging each picture with the words that best describe the collection. This provides an easy way to find images when building a seasonal catwalk report. Printing all the catwalk thumbnails was commonplace in the past, and some agencies and design studios still prefer print. Using new technology with tagging services will save you time and is more environmentally friendly. There are many photo editing programs that will help you to organize and tag images accordingly.

Tagging Examples

The following are some sample tags you can use to tag images. Once your image collection gets bigger, it would also be good practice to tag seasonal information. In order to remember and find images quickly and easily, always tag using the same words every season and use your dedicated dictionary of words.

4.10–4.11
Tagging images will help in finding similar images from various catwalks. Here, with Ann Demeulemeester and Comme des Garçons, the mood tag was 'modern gothic'.

4.10

1. **Mood:** For mood tags, use words that evoke the spirit of the feeling of the collection: festive, somber, intelligent, sporty, street, punk, gothic, ethnic, young, mature, elegant etc.

 2. **Key Looks:** Use a key look tag followed by tags such as office, two-piece, three-piece, cyber, outdoor, holiday, boho etc.

3. **Silhouette:** Start building your silhouette dictionary with words such as slim, semi-slim, loose, slouchy, volume, short etc. You can also tag with descriptive words that influence the shape, such as padded or quilted.

 4. **Construction:** Use terms such as tailored, draped, raw, deconstructed, smocked etc. Sometimes it is hard to see exactly how a garment is constructed, but you can tag at least your impression of it with the construction tag.

5. **Surface:** This includes jacquard, slogans, numbers and specific colours such as red, white, black, orange, mauve etc. The surface tags can be numerous and can be updated season after season.

6. **Accessories:** There are many descriptive words to use for footwear and bags. You should first tag them with construction information. In other words, what type of shoes are in question: boots, sneakers, sandals? Shoe tags include high-tops, trainers, construction boot, wingtips, thick soles, boots, pointy, alligator. Key items can then be tagged with other descriptive tags, such as mood or surface. Bag types can be clutch, backpack, briefcase, document folder, shopper etc. Tag the types with mood and other words, as well. The tags should be as descriptive as possible to help you systematically detect trends in catwalks.

It is important to collect as many images as possible after the season is over in order to have a selection of data to pull from. If tagged correctly, all images with a specific mood will come up when you put a mood word into the search box of your photo organizer. (Remember to also tag the season.)

4.11

4.12

4.13

4.14

4.15

4.12
Key looks are usually the strongest looks of the collection.

4.13
Silhouette is often referenced in catwalk reviews. Here is the Craig Green spring/summer 2017 collection with a new take on a more volume-rich menswear silhouette.

4.14
Construction is sometimes difficult to ascertain from images, but basic terms such as 'tailored' and 'deconstructed' are often used to describe menswear.

4.15
Surface design elements, such as graphics, are easier to categorize when tagged.

CHERRY COMPOTE
Winter fruit inspires this sweet, sticky shade of red-pink, expressing a masc-femme dimension.

4.16

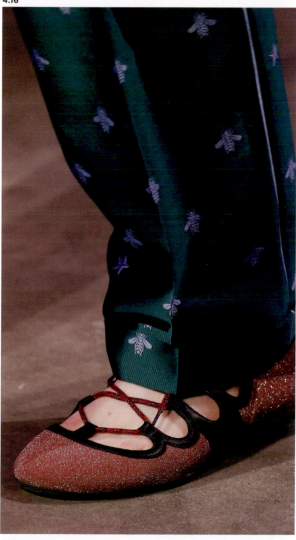
4.17

TAGGING EXERCISE

- Download free photo organizer software and catwalk images from London, Milan, Paris and New York.
- Each collection on average should be thirty images, giving you over 100 images to work with.
- Start tagging images first by season, using a standard abbreviation for each season (e.g., A/W15) or whatever you prefer. It is important to use the same system throughout.
- Continue tagging with keywords that cover all the areas of Mood, Silhouette, Construction, Surface and Accessories. Use a Key Look tag only on an item that you consider to be the main look or piece of the collection.
- Tag each image with at least five tags. In the end, see what combination of words are tagged most.
- Can you detect a trend from your tag analysis?
- In this exercise, you have tagged several collections with these words. When you include trade show and street style coverage, you will have a statistical system to detect several seasonal trends.

4.16
Colour can also be categorized and be part of the surface design and is one of the most important parts of close-to-season catwalk reporting.

4.17
Footwear can be tagged not only by type but also to suggest mood. Here, tags would be flat, gillie, ballerina, glitter, feminine, romantic, dandy, slipper, Edwardian.

STREET STYLE ANALYSIS

Street style analysis has become one of the most featured sources of seasonal menswear information and inspiration. Images are used for styling suggestions and customer profile inspiration. Street style is a democratic medium. Anybody can be a model, giving style and trends a more human quality. When analyzing street style we can use the same methodology and systems we use in catwalk analysis; however, breakdown of street style is slightly different. Key looks are more difficult to pinpoint because it is not really a commercial realm. Street style provides an important flavour and feel for a venue, whether it's outside a catwalk show, inside a trade show, or on city streets. For example, Milan street style will differ from London street style (in general), with both having many inspirational and individual looks.

Fashion-driven events, such as music festivals and trade shows of various types, also provide valuable street style information. There are many channels available for obtaining this information, but first-hand experience is the best. If there is a fashion event in your city, go to the event (equipped with a camera) to experience the street scene yourself.

Street style offers inspirational material that brands use for direction in collection buying and sometimes even design. Therefore, it is important to comment on what were the main points of the look and which looks were seen in all the cities.

For street style analysis the main factors to consider are key styles, silhouette, surface and accessories.

4.18
Street style coverage is still important for inspirational styling ideas as seen here at Pitti Uomo, Florence (the most photographed menswear trade event in the world).

4.19
Street style analysis can be quite specific as it is with the length of this coat or robe by Pigalle, signalling the possible future length direction of overcoats.

4.18

KEY STYLES

Key styles can be categorized in the same way as menswear; for example, street style can be young, mature, sporty or a hybrid of various menswear styles. Key style also refers to styling and how various looks are put together; the strongest of these will direct the next few seasons in menswear styling. Key styles do not have to be extravagant and can be very paired down.

After analyzing the street style scene, you will also start to recognize the personal style of the photographers. In order to get a sense of the key styles for the season, view the main street style photographers' online reports via websites such as tommyton .com, thousandyardstyle.com, guerreisms.com and streetper.com.

SILHOUETTE

Silhouette is as important for menswear as it is for womenswear. The best way to understand the menswear silhouette is simply to look at as many images as possible and see if there is a prevailing volume. Glean from street photography the variations that are on offer. For example, are shoulders getting bigger or is the soft shoulder still important? What is happening with the trouser width and length? Is it short and narrow or long and narrow or long and wide? The silhouette analysis can also be about specific items, such as coats or the silhouette and shape of accessories (thick soles, larger bags etc.).

4.19

COLOUR AND GRAPHICS

Surface design in street style mainly refers to the print and colour of the garments and accessories. In street style analysis, categorize the main colours, print, appliqué and graphics seen in the images, in order to get an idea about what the main directions are. Graphics and the type of print should also be categorized and analysed. What type of print is seen the most for the season? What type of graphics (such as T-shirt graphics) are men wearing? And what colours are the most prominent in the season's street style coverage?

FOOTWEAR AND ACCESSORIES

Street style coverage also pays great attention to footwear and accessories. All the previously mentioned street style photographers often photograph interesting shoes and bags, as well as other accessories such as sunglasses and neckwear. Again, styling is an important part of the coverage reporting the latest ways to wear menswear. One recent street-style-triggered trend was a winter gilet/blazer combination. This drove a blazer trend with a removable quilted shell, which is part of today's menswear offer from Hugo Boss to Marks and Spencer. Another recent street-style-triggered trend is the focus on men's hats, especially classic types such as fedoras.

4.20
Street-style photography is an effective way to monitor and research the latest directions in menswear surface graphics. Here, a shot from Japanese journalist Yu Masui during London Collections Men in 2016.

4.20

4.21

4.22

4.21
Interesting patch
placement makes
this jacket a good
inspirational piece
for brands to
consider new and
alternate ways to
impact the surface.

4.22
Shoes and other
accessories are
often covered
in street-style
photography.

TRADE SHOW ANALYSIS

Fashion media do not usually cover trade shows, making it a good opportunity to collect information that is not easily available to others. It is not easy to find trade show reports online, since the shows are only for trade professionals and not public information. Magazines such as *WeAr* and *Collezioni* that have good information from trade shows will appear too late for professional purposes.

There are two ways to approach a trade show: as a student or as a professional. Trend agencies usually send someone to cover the shows, or they hire a scout to gather information. Students are usually granted access to the shows on the last day. If you have accreditation to visit a show, then you can get a more detailed in-stand experience (depending on the stand, of course). To get a good idea what the season will be offering, it is best to visit as many shows as possible in person.

When visiting a trade show, base your research on the same parameters as you do your catwalk and street style analysis. Look at the main characteristics appearing in various brands. Look for, first and foremost, some level of innovation. Brands are fighting to get attention in these shows and always try to bring something new to buyers. When doing coverage and analyzing trade shows, look for the following: key items, fabrication, colour and graphics.

KEY ITEMS

Since the trade show environment is a little harder to navigate, with stands often only open to buyers, it is good to walk around and get a general impression of the atmosphere. When visiting a stand, try to understand what type of brand it is. The best way is to look for important articles that brands are pushing – the ones that are displayed in the stand more prominently. In addition to this, stands sometimes use extravagant items to attract attention to bring buyers and press to the stand. Another way to understand the brand is to ask what the iconic pieces or the best sellers are.

FABRICATION

Fabrication is an action or process of manufacturing or inventing something.

Trade shows are a great way to see items close up, in order to understand the items better. Touching the garments will give you so much more information than an image will provide. Look for new surface treatments, washes and materials used in manufacturing. Trade shows, such as ISPO, which specialize in performance and sportswear, are full of new material innovations. Also, menswear trade shows often have areas that specialize in outerwear or sportswear that may show new fabrication opportunities.

4.23

4.24

4.23
Stand displays often tell what the key items or the main looks are that the brands are pushing, as seen here with Chasin' brand.

4.24
Always look for new surface treatments, such as the cracked paint effect on this Eleven Paris top.

COLOUR

There are always a few colours that are immediately apparent in trade shows. After walking around it is good to take note of which are the most prominent colours displayed in or outside stands. This will make a good starting point for further in-depth research. Depending on the brand, garments are not always displayed in all colours available. Usually the strongest expected colour sellers are displayed.

GRAPHICS

Graphics in past seasons have seen a huge increase in apparel, from T-shirts to outerwear to accessories. Print and graphic communication has been huge, especially in streetwear. When considering graphics, it is important to look for the type of graphic surface motifs used. Camouflage and florals are always present, as are types of plaid. Consider the seasonal updates of these classic prints, as well as how much of it is used in clothing. Beyond the classics, look also for the different types of T-shirt prints: are they humorous or nostalgic? Do they use slogans? Also take note of general themes in graphics. Are they referring to the theme of the overall collection or are they just decorative treatments?

4.25

4.26

4.27

4.25
Fessura displays
two colour options
for this particular
sneaker model in
Pitti Uomo.

4.26
Trade shows offer a
wealth of material
for print and
graphic research, as
seen here from Rich
Kids label.

4.27
Graphics are one
of the best ways to
create a content-
rich trade show
report. Look for
which types, prints
and slogans are
used in the shows.
Eleven Paris stand.

STUDENT SHOWS

Student catwalks are valuable for their visionary quality because they are not tied to a selling season. Student catwalks, or end-of-degree catwalks, take place in late spring in May or June. Colleges such as Central Saint Martins in the UK and Antwerp Fashion Academy in Belgium are on the fashion radar, with international fashion houses looking to them for the next big name. One of the largest student shows is London's graduate fashion week (www.gfw.org.uk). Because these shows display the work of future designers, they are perfect venues to gather early trend signals.

4.28
Student graduate work is closely watched by fashion insiders. Here is RISD graduate Adam Dalton Blake.

4.29
Graduate catwalks provide an important window to the future of menswear and provide a good starting point for trend research. London Graduate Fashion week winner Hannah Wallace.

4.28

4.29

COLOUR ANALYSIS ASSIGNMENT

- Scan through the current season's menswear shows, from London Collections Men to New York Men's fashion week.
- Select about ten brands that stand out for you and write down five to ten key colours per brand.
- If one of the colours (or similar shades) appears in more than three brands in various cities, it is possibly a colour trend. However, this is just a start for the research, since you will cross reference trade shows and street style.
- After you have focused on four or five colour trends, find more evidence by going through the catwalks again with your colour 'key'.
- Look into the season's trade show coverage to find further evidence of the colour.
- Finally, search the street-style images for that same season online to conclude your research.
- The colour information does not only come from clothes, but can also be found in bags, shoes and other accessories.
- After deciding on each colour, look for its reference numbers from companies such as Pantone.
- At the end of the exercise, create a PDF with the four or five colour stories. Give each colour and trend a good editorial title, creating a content-rich and inspiring project.
- Present to class.

4.30

DAVID EDGAR
CEO BDA London

David Edgar is one of the founding partners of Bureaux Design Associates (BDA). For the past 25 years he has helped to steer the creative team and the overall business strategy for the business. BDA specializes in branding, graphic design and helping companies with long-term strategy, including product and trend adaptation. David also oversees the menswear content for *View* magazine, a leader in materials, colour and trend direction for brands and designers alike. David Edgar's experience in menswear encompasses all areas, from design to retail.

What is your past and how did you get where you are now? I studied fashion design and gained a degree from Liverpool University. I specialized in menswear and, after moving to London thirty-five years ago, I was a practicing menswear designer for different high street retailers and brands. With three other partners we set about establishing an agency providing apparel design, brand and marketing for the fashion industry. Back in those days neither retailers nor brands employed in-house designers and so we were 'contract for hire'!

During those early days there were a lot of things happening in the creative industry, in music, publishing, art and, of course, fashion. At the time it all seemed normal, but, looking back and beyond those times, it was pretty revolutionary.

What does your agency BDA do? Now nearly every retailer and brand have strong design teams in-house and we always work alongside them. We are often appointed by senior management to help to steer their corporate strategy . . . helping bring together design, buying, merchandising and marketing. Our twenty-strong design team have to be much more strategic in the way they think, which is the role of an outside agency and should never be the role of an in-house team. It's our role to give context to the content and vice versa. Much easier looking in than looking out.

What is your role with the *View* menswear magazine? We are still working with David Shah, the publisher of *View* magazine, after twenty-five years, when we helped launch the first issue. At the time there were lots of new publications coming to market, like *The Face*. We wanted *View* to be new and different, which it was; there was nothing like it when it launched. It got a great reception. Today David Shah still believes in the magazine in paper form, and we are looking at investing in more ideas to make the 'paper' as relevant as it was when it first launched.

We often are in long workshops with our clients, with sometimes twenty or thirty people in at a time. The designers and buyers all still bring in magazines or

4.30
David Edgar is the owner and head of Bureaux Design Associates (BDA) and has worked with his agency in every global territory over the past 25 years.

4.31
BDA provides strong colour direction for *View* magazine.

4.32
BDA works with *View* on menswear trend stories.

tear sheets. I've never seen one try to show trends on their mobile phone! We are looking forward to new opportunities and maybe new products under the *View* brand to continue to keep it fresh.

How do you get to your trends? There is no starting point and no finishing point; it's just all about research, research and more research. A continual cycle of putting you and your team out there, keeping your network and your travels as wide as possible and drawing from any area that gives you direction.

How has the world of trend forecasting changed in the past years? We can see, through the difficult trading periods - the world's high street going through tough times and the whole climate everyone is living in – that the 'essentials' product is what everyone is focusing on. Updating classics with broad appeal and maximum efficiencies in fabric and styling. The whole seasonal trend thing is pretty much a thing of the past – although hot weather does need lighter clothes than colder weather does! But we are always researching new product opportunities through the trading periods and work especially hard in what used to called the transitional periods (between hot and cold weather).

There is so much 'trend' information out there and much of it is free, if you look around. We went into high street stores the other day and everyone had done the 1970s look. It was absolutely evident that 'trend' is no longer the differentiator . . . it's much more about the brand's personality – how it talks to its customer and what the brand stands for is going to be the difference between success and failure.

What is the role of forecasting in your strategic partnership with companies? We always do lots of research into market and customer. We need to know what the customer is looking for through analysis of the sales and other research tools that can tell you what the customer is searching for rather than relying on the team's intuitive process. It's no longer good enough to have a buyer with a good eye for product!

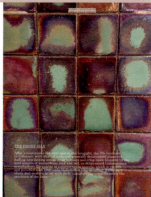

4.31   4.32

CHAPTER SUMMARY

In this chapter we have outlined the information to collect for both short and long-term trend analysis. Short-term analysis relates to 'close-to-selling-season' information (next season), while long-term information will be in three to four seasons' time. The same methods of collecting information can be applied to both short and long-term trend information.

We have also discussed what to look for on catwalks and have reviewed the importance of trade shows, exploring the differences between finished product trade shows and material trade shows. The importance of street style imagery as one of the most popular forms of communication in fashion today keeps it relevant for analysis and forecasting; it provides guidance for many aspects of marketing, especially a close-to-season strategy, as street style deals mainly with already available collections.

HOMEWORK ASSIGNMENTS

1. Review the latest collections for menswear and point out the key looks for a collection. Look for the one that, in your opinion, encapsulates the collection best or might be the best seller.
2. Have a look at menswear collections in an online runway portal or a collections magazine, and select a designer. See if you can spot a general theme for the collection. Give the mood a word that describes it best. Do the same with a few designers and review the assortment of words that might describe them.

DISCUSSION ACTIVITIES AND PROJECTS

1. Look at the recent menswear footwear silhouette and details from Milan, London and from Paris. What differences can you spot?
2. Write a small report describing details and the mood of the menswear season (including all the cities in one report). (Do not use images.)
3. Research street style and note which graphics trends you can spot for the current season.

KEY WORDS
catwalk
close-to-selling-season
exit
fabrication
key looks
surface design

5.1

5.1
Research is
gathered from
accumulated
sources and then
filtered to provide
a base for the
forecast.

5

How to Research Trends

LEARNING OBJECTIVES

- Define 'research'.
- Understand what and how to research.
- Analyse cultural starting points.
- Differentiate various types of research.
- Compare different types of trade shows.
- Evaluate data gathering techniques.

INTRODUCTION

In trend forecasting we are not initially researching one particular area of interest, but gathering information on as many areas as possible. Even in fashion, one needs to be aware of what is happening in areas as diverse as politics and the economy. These areas are intertwined and ultimately influence fashion. Politics directly influences society and economics, which will ultimately influence spending. At times of economic uncertainty, spending goes down and also becomes more concentrated on essentials. It is vital to conduct research in order to be able to make well-supported, directional suggestions for a trend, which will be the basis of your presentations (see Chapter 6). The better and more substantial your research, the better your foresight will be.

Trend research is generally gathered from various sources, then filtered, accumulated and analysed systematically by categorizing information. As a trend forecaster you are trying to tap into the early signals that are bubbling just under the surface, or manifesting themselves in the fringes of culture or fashion. Therefore, it is important to research new ideas and innovative directions in thinking. However, this does not mean that trends are only about new products. They can also be a new adoption of old ideas. Trends are often cumulative in nature, meaning that trend research can also involve the investigation of old ideas with new added information.

Research is the most important part of the trend process. Thorough research will provide a credible foundation for the trend product– in this case, the forecast or the analysis. Good first-hand research will add value to your analysis and prediction. The initial decision that determines the starting point of your research depends on whether you are analyzing the close-to-season trends or predicting something further away in the future (see Chapter 4). Although trend forecasting is the observing and gathering of information, which is then evaluated in order to make

5.2
Trend research is generally gathered from various sources, such as current events and lifestyle magazines, then filtered and analysed.

predictions and not to support a personal point of view, it cannot be completely objective. The information collected can inspire you to present the work with your signature or style.

A trend forecaster should be a sponge who absorbs all kinds of information – regardless of personal interest – and curiosity is a key characteristic: don't forget that anything and everything can be an early signal of trends.

5.2

BASICS AND DEFINITIONS

There are two types of research: primary and secondary. Primary research is first-hand information and raw data that is recorded personally. Secondary research entails using existing information or research, such as reviewing reports, print or editorial material from a menswear magazine.

Primary research can involve gathering physical information, such as taking a photo of a jacket or a hat, collecting a swatch of suiting material from a trade show, or drawing a quick silhouette of something. It can also involve questionnaires, surveys or interviews with individual people. Survey questions can be broken down into two main types: closed-ended and open-ended. Closed-ended questions limit the interviewee's ability to respond by having a list of answers they must choose from (multiple choice). For example, if you were studying the next retail season, you might ask a closed-ended question:

What type of jeans will you be most likely buy next season?
A. Bootcut
B. Elephant leg
C. Skinny
D. Straight leg

Open-ended questions do not have a list of answers to choose from and allow the subject to answer with personal opinion. The answers to this type of question are more difficult to statistically analyse but provide more information when studying general mindsets and purchase moods. An example of an open-ended question is: what is your opinion of denim jeans? Or, even more specifically: list the types of denim jeans that you are planning to purchase this coming year and why. There are many types of questions one can ask, but a combination of closed-ended and open-ended questions make a good trend survey.

It is also important to test a survey to make sure it will provide usable results. The best way to do this is to test it with a few friends first. Create a small questionnaire to test on your friends and see if the survey produces acceptable results.

QUALITATIVE RESEARCH

Qualitative research investigates attitudes, reasons, motivations and opinions. The research questions are often open-ended, asking questions that can be answered by a short description. This type of research asks questions about lifestyle and general behaviour in order to reveal a bigger picture for analysis, paving the way for quantitative research. This type of information is very useful when trying to understand the customer more deeply, as it is used to gain an understanding of underlying reasons, opinions and motivations.

Qualitative research can be conducted using focus groups or with face-to-face interviews. It is also possible to collect qualitative data through observational field studies, where men's behaviour and/or choice in clothes are recorded in a specific location (e.g., in a shop or in the street). These methods provide valuable support and are an integral part of trend analysis and prediction. Although many companies rely heavily on statistics, qualitative research is an invaluable tool for forecasting.

QUANTITATIVE RESEARCH

Quantitative research gathers data that is turned into statistical measurable information. It is often done with surveys that can be conducted online or through face-to-face interviews. The questions should be specific and clear, with controlled and limited answers: What colour trousers will you most likely be buying next season? These responses can be turned into numerical results (e.g., 63 per cent chose black as the most likely colour to invest in). If a brand wants to know information on sunglasses trends, you would ask specific questions relating to sunglasses, perhaps referencing the type of specific shapes men will most likely invest in.

Quantitative research will allow you to gather some raw data on which to base your further research and will support and add further credibility to your reporting, which is especially important in a corporate environment.

GATHERING OF DATA

When considering what information to gather, you should initially look at news and current events. The socioeconomic and political climate will help you set a solid foundation on which to build your research. If you know what is happening around you in a non-fashion environment, the fashion will follow. It is important to remember that trends are very specific to the geographical and cultural location; for example, a trend forecast made for Scandinavia would not necessarily be suitable for the Middle East. Although men in general have a way of dressing that can work in various geographical regions, sometimes cultural factors do need to be taken into consideration. When gathering data, consider advances in science and technology, or developments in materials and manufacturing, in order to imagine what could have an impact. Although it would be difficult to make a specific menswear trend analysis or prediction from such a vast information pool, it is important to have a solid knowledge of the world around you – not only of menswear-related information.

Fashion and menswear are cultural aspects of society. Therefore, research may include, but not be limited to, art, music, cinema, literature, product design, architecture, interiors, exhibitions, trade shows, retail, food, fashion, photography and performance arts. Menswear, and fashion in general, reacts to what is happening in culture. Designers are inspired by cultural aspects and consumers are directly affected by this. If the designs are relevant and speak to the consumer, they will part with their cash. As a trend forecaster, you need to be able to have a broad understanding of culture, yet be able to use information that is quite specific, rather than general. Clients like to have confident, precise information to work with that will result in measurable outcomes.

WHERE TO DO RESEARCH

The initial stage of research involves an exploration of the creative cultural signals of the moment (e.g., what exhibitions are being talked about, what movies people are watching, what people are reading and posting about). It is important to explore these experiences in person or virtually in order to see if you can sense early signals that could evolve into a stronger trend. For menswear research, you would start by looking into sports, travel, music, retail, food, TV, cinema, catwalks and street style. The latter stages of investigation should focus more on trade shows and in-store product – information can sometimes be found in non-fashion industries, but more often in trade shows, such as material shows. What you are doing is trying to understand whether there are connecting points among all the various research experiences in which you are participating. Trend research can be hugely overwhelming because of the amount of information we are exposed to, but focusing on a category such as menswear will narrow it down.

USING THE INTERNET FOR TREND RESEARCH

The Internet is often the first stop when starting to research a topic or gathering general information. The Internet can provide many useful tools for helping with trend research, such as Google Alerts and Google Trends. Google Alerts is a tool that tracks programmed words, so every time the word is published on the Internet you will receive a notification. Google Trends is a service that shows the subjects that are trending at that moment and the search history of keywords. It also allows you to see which fashion brands are searched the most and at what times of the year. Museums, national archives, institutes, guilds and expert websites, such as *Scientific American*, *National Geographic* and *Scenario*, are also good sources.

It is advisable when carrying out Internet-based research to take the research to a deeper level and not just settle for the first level of information. Everyone has access to Internet sources, so get beyond what everyone reads. Online fashion communicators such Diane Pernet and websites such as Showstudio.com provide a wealth of inspirational information. However, when you read something online, look at its references and see if those sources are available online or in a library for further research. This can provide more leads and further reading material for your exploration – and exploring various paths is always useful.

5.3

5.3
The latest material innovations in other industries can also be brought into fashion. Vantablack is the world's blackest black, used in space and defence sectors. Vantablack is not used in clothing yet, but will be eventually, according to the company.

The Internet provides valuable reading material that is easily accessible and often free. Platforms such as JSTOR and various free digital libraries, such as the Gutenberg Project and Google Books, are good places to find further reading, in addition to college libraries. Most college libraries have open databases for catalogue research, making them a good free resource. Having access to a library is critical to obtaining good first-hand information because library image research can add value to your project.

The Internet is an endless pool of material, yet it should be used with care: always verify the authenticity of the source material. That's another good reason to dive into the references and sources that were used by the author of what you've read. If there are no reliable links or print references, you may need to disregard that source.

5.5

ART

Contemporary art is of contemporary culture; therefore, it can be a great barometer of society, mirroring what is happening in sociocultural life. Art can be in the form of images, film, performance, textiles or a way of life – art can be everything and anything. Interest in art has increased, with museums offering more and more crowd-pulling exhibitions. Museums may offer additional access with online galleries that can provide a wealth of material for research. Art is inspiring.

The presentation of work, whether in the form of an installation, painting, film or drawing, will provide new clues and early direction for your research. Observe the style of art that is being discussed and exhibited – for example, abstract expressionism, minimal, light, contemporary. For example,

5.4
There are many sources for secondary research on the Internet, such as *Scenario* magazine, JSTOR and various design portals and blogs.

5.5
Diane Pernet's portal, A Shaded View on Fashion, is widely read among the fashion insiders. It documents the up-and-coming fashion and design scene.

5.4

if 'light' art exhibitions, such as London's Lumiere of 2016 and James Turrell's LACMA retrospective, get international coverage, they can influence designers and popular culture. This is something you would want to notice and tap into before anybody else. What a forecaster needs to know are the general directions and nuances of artistic expression. Art can be beneficial in many ways – visually inspirational and an aid in storytelling. A mood can be expressed effectively with the help of art, whether it is classical or contemporary.

Art is also shown in more commerce-focused shows, such as Frieze Art or Art Basel. Although they are commercial shows, they are valuable in providing a sense of the art market. Art and cultural events, such as the Venice Biennale or Documenta (every five years), also offer opportunities to understand art as a global and creative, rather than a consumer, phenomena. However, both types of art shows can provide a platform to further develop your research.

Magazines, blogs, journals, zines and the street are all resources containing material that will be relevant to the moment and can be used in the forecasting process.

5.6

5.7

5.6
Art Basel is one of the most prestigious art shows in the world, visited by many designers and art lovers alike.

5.7
The Venice Art Biennale is inspirational in many senses, as seen here at the 2015 British pavilion.

5.8

5.9

PRINT

Printed materials include magazines, books, catalogues and flyers. Magazines are an important source for a trend forecaster, not only for product content, but also for styling and editorial opinions. Magazines can influence and trigger major fashion trends. Exhibition literature, usually free printed pamphlets, will often have information that can help with your research, even if you do not purchase a full exhibition catalogue. You'll need the basic exhibition information when citing your research sources.

In the more mainstream and commercial realm, the 'Top 10' book charts and book reviews will provide an insight into current interests. What people are reading, especially in non-fiction, can indicate general levels of interest. This is also internationally thought provoking; the 'must-read' books often vary between cultures.

5.8
Erwin Wurm work is often full of humour, bloated forms and inspiring colour.

5.9
Belgian designer Walter Van Beirendonck collaborated with Erwin Wurm on his spring/summer 2012 collection titled Cloud # 9.

5.10
Literary phenomena can spark a trend, as the Beats did while paving the way to Hippie counter culture.

5.10

Although books and the way we consume literature has changed, a bestseller book list is still a good starting point to understand what people are reading. It was certainly the case that literature once influenced menswear, as in the Beat generation, where a movement was founded on a type of literary expression. Although direct menswear influences are not as prominent today in literature, as a cultural starting point literature certainly can help with trend formation. Looking at the London Book Fair, Frankfurt Book Show or Hay-on-Wye festival may provide ideas as to what people are reading or will read. Most literary festivals and trade shows also have web portals offering a wealth of information about the themes of the shows.

5.12

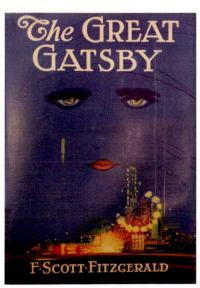

5.11

5.11
Classics such as *The Great Gatsby*, seen here at the London International Antiquarian Book Fair, are often turned into blockbuster films, which was part of the reason for the increased interest in classic menswear styles after 2013.

5.12
In May 2013, when *The Great Gatsby* movie was released, the e-book sold over 185,000 copies. In June 2013 several Gatsby-inspired looks were seen.

interested in. Pop stars often wear attention-grabbing outfits in videos and public appearances, triggering possible trends. Today's music scene presents a full package that includes styling and publicity (graphics and communication that can trigger graphics trends); bands have become branded products.

Some of the greatest youth fashion spectacles are music festivals and gigs. In fact many trend agencies and fashion magazines cover them in order to get up-to-date styling and direction information. The hip hop scene, for example, has influenced menswear in the past decades, from styling to graphics. Examples are Run-D.M.C. with their Kangol hat and gold chain looks that influenced the early hip hop generation. Currently one cannot ignore the influence of Kanye West's Yeezy label, which is closely intertwined with his music, especially after the colossal album release/fashion show extravaganza at the sold-out Madison Square Garden event in 2016.

MUSIC

Music, and especially the pop music scene, can influence fashion. Musicians such as Elvis, the Beatles, David Bowie and Sid Vicious all impacted men's fashions and trends. Researching the music scene (such as festivals and videos) may provide directional information regarding what younger demographics are

MOVING IMAGE

Film is an emotive medium that influences people the world over, including fashion designers. Inspiration can come from cinema that will filter to society in various ways. Film festivals are a good place to see new influential films. IMDB, the international movie database, will feature what movies are in production in their 'coming soon' section. In order to be ahead of the consumer, these early glimpses may provide you with possible trend influencers before the movies are released. The movie industry is influential on many levels as a trend creator or as a driver of fashion trends. One good example is *Avatar* (2009); it raised the bar for 3D entertainment in theatres as well as homes. John Travolta's character, Tony Manero, in *Saturday Night Fever* (1977) initiated the global Disco craze with suited no-tie looks. New York's famed Studio 54 opened the same year, fuelling a few years of the Saturday Night Fever look at the end of the 1970s. Another example from the past is Richard Gere's character Julian in *American Gigolo* (1980). The film performance triggered the lightweight Armani suit look for men, which defined the decade. *Easy Rider* (1969) is still often referred to when the US denim biker trend reappears in the marketplace. Movie culture today translates to T-shirt graphics with various superhero references (e.g., the Marvel, DC, or Star Wars characters). Movies, just like

other art forms, signal the spirit of the times.

Today, TV is perhaps even more important than cinema. One of the recent influential TV shows is *Mad Men*. Most of the menswear magazines, such as *Esquire* and *GQ*, featured editorials and reviews of the 1960s-inspired sleek looks, including statement pieces and colours. This program brought *Mad Men* references not only to editorials but also to advertising, styling and, especially, interiors. In a 2015 article in the *LA Times*, the trend was discussed in great detail as it influenced the interior design business. Speaking of Crate & Barrel and West Elm, 'it was Don Draper's workplace and penthouse that resonated most powerfully, bringing mid-century modernism back into the mass-market mainstream and becoming a form of design shorthand' (Keeps 2015).

5.14

5.13
David Bowie was a style icon for whom music and personal expression through dress were inextricably linked.

5.14
Television and cinema influence the menswear market from visual merchandising to the end product. Don Draper, the main character in *Mad Men*, started menswear clothing trends as well as interior trends.

5.15

PRODUCT DESIGN

The relationship between product design and fashion has a special interaction. Product designers are often looking at fashion lifestyles to create something desirable, while fashion looks to product for innovations in materials and colour. Wearable products also influence clothing design (portable player pockets etc.). Trend forecasters often use product references in their mood boards to widen the understanding of where trends come from and how they can connect to fashion. The Internet has several product design portals that feature the latest must-have items. A product can support the trend

5.15
Tokujin Yoshioka during Salone del Mobile often presents new products in a fully immersive environment, as seen here in the Moroso Showroom work titled 'Twilight'.

vision very well since it allows an opportunity to 'objectify' a trend; an object makes a trend something tangible and easy to understand.

Many trends can be identified in product design events such as Salone del Mobile or London Design Week. Graduate shows, such as that of the Royal College of Art, will also showcase the latest innovation in product design. Milan's Salone del Mobile is the most important design festival in the world, where it is possible to see a range of design innovation, from student work to major brands. The show is mainly a furniture fair, but the expression of space is often explored with such designers as Tokujin Yoshioka or Patricia Urquiola. The London Design festival also often crosses over to art, as illustrated by the recent interactive Audi-sponsored robotics performance called Outrace, in addition to other installations by numerous international design stars such as Philippe Starck and Marc Newson.

ARCHITECTURE

Our habitat and style of living changes much more slowly than fashion because buildings take longer to construct than clothing. Observing architecture can be an interesting source of inspiration. For example, the new BBC London and *New York Times* buildings both embrace transparency in their own ways. The BBC studios are built around one enormous central open space with no clear hierarchy, while the *New York Times* skyscraper is a huge glass house where you can literally see through the building. We live today in a world where transparency is key. This trend has also crossed over to other fields, especially in relation to corporate social responsibility (e.g., in fashion, the disclosure of product origin and production practices). Some design hotels even have transparent (or opaque) doors or walls to the bathrooms – previously a completely private and enclosed space.

Architecture is a vital part of trend forecasting because metaphorical associations can be made (e.g., clothing as the house for our bodies). Artists such as Ervin Wurm use structure and clothing as their mixed media, merging dress and art.

5.16

INTERIORS

Interiors are far more personal and quicker to adapt to change than architecture; they are a type of personal showroom that can reflect the taste and social status of the owner. In clothing we often want something new very quickly. Interiors are not quite as demanding; however, interior design magazines are still full of new trends for the home. The possibility of changing interiors has been made much easier and more affordable for more people by companies such as Ikea. In the case of trend research, the interior can provide a mood reference or a styling direction. Interior design publications and blogs provide endless sources of inspiration.

RETAIL

The retail environment provides an opportunity to review not only products but also consumer behaviour. It is important to research the leading menswear retailers in the world and to observe their merchandising. Many trend agencies cover major cities' leading window displays, and the retail environment is often a featured section in publications such as *Sportswear International* and *WeAr*. Retailers are also constantly searching for new ways to sell product in order to stay ahead of the competition. One such idea is the guerrilla shop or pop-up shopping. Since online shopping is enjoying exponential growth each year, brick-and-mortar retail needs to be completely re-thought, even beyond the pop-up phenomenon.

5.16
Salone Internazionale del Mobile in Milan is the most important event in the international design calendar because of the size of the event and the calibre of design houses present.

5.17
Retail, especially window merchandising as seen here in Colette, Paris, can provide inspiration for your research.

5.17

COLOUR RESEARCH

Trade shows are an essential contributor to colour research. It is fundamental to understand the concept of colour before attempting colour forecasting. There are numerous colour theories; those of Sir Isaac Newton and Johann Wolfgang von Goethe are the most important. Isaac Newton's famous seventeenth-century experiments with light and prism brought understanding to what colour actually is. While Newton focused on the spectrum of colour, Goethe focused on the perception of colour as well as the emotional language of colour. Joseph Albers' *Interaction of Color* (1963/2006) provides essential information on how colours react next to one another. Knowing how well colours will work with one another is basic knowledge that is required before suggesting colours to a client. Some are extremely pleasant to the eye, while others can create disturbing kinetic visual effects. Derek Jarman's (2010) *Chroma* provides a valuable insight into the emotional effects for colour and explores how colour can be described far more effectively than just by its commonly used name.

In trend forecasting the focus is often on the emotional or emotive content of the colour and the ability to match it with the trend. The most straightforward way to do this is to select an image that summarizes the trend and pick colours from it. For example, if the trend is wintry and gothic, a colour story with primary bright colours would not make sense.

Traditionally, colour use has been limited to dark muted colours for autumn/winter, with lighter versions of the same colours for spring/summer. The colour use for menswear differs greatly depending on where you are geographically and culturally. In India, for example, menswear colour use is completely different from that in Canada. In the warmer climates, people are far more inclined to wear seasonless clothes (e.g., with lighter colour palettes for heat absorption or cultural reasons). In the western fashion world, there have been more and more new colours slowly moving into menswear, signalling that men are becoming more comfortable using colour in their wardrobe. This is apparent in catwalks, but even more visible in mainstream retail. Pop colours in menswear are being used more, and even full-colour items are becoming more common. The winter colours and the summer colours are also overlapping, creating brand new opportunities for menswear trends.

There are some basics regarding colour and material that need to be considered. When there is a smaller area of colour, the colour looks darker, and when the surface is bigger, the colour appears lighter. This is something you need to consider when looking at colour samples in a leather trade show, for example. Often in trade shows the material is shown as larger pieces accompanied by smaller swatches.

Colour may also appear to be different among materials – for example, the same colour blue may look like different shades when appearing on a paper, a natural textile and a synthetic. Leather is especially problematic because it is organic and can show great differences between animal hides. There are colour matching systems which can help reduce these problems. The Pantone colour system is one of the most widely used colour referencing systems in the world. How to use colour information in a presentation is covered in Chapter 6.

5.18
Colour is one of the main focus areas for brands. It is important to understand the seasonal nuances and cultural trends that will influence colour.

5.18

RUNWAY CONFIRMATION   Current Season

John Elliott   Stampd   Etudes   Officine Generale   Fendi

5.19

FASHION: CATWALKS

Fashion shows are essential for menswear trend analysis. Retailers the world over follow the direction and cues that the shows offer. Menswear fashion week shows take place before womenswear shows, which means that menswear presentations are the first opportunity to see new season directions. As the first seasonal reporting for fashion is menswear, it holds a very important place in the fashion calendar. This is the earliest opportunity to see new season colours, materials and silhouettes, as well as key items such as shoes and accessories. Many of the trends seen on menswear shows will also appear in womenswear, since designers often use the same inspiration for both collections.

The first menswear runway shows for the season are in London with the London Collections: Men presentation, followed by the Pitti Uomo trade show in Florence. After Pitti is Milan's menswear fashion week, followed by Paris and New York. There is also trade show activity in New York and Berlin, which offer apparel geared toward men. The London Collection: Men is the most creative, young and forward thinking out of the three fashion weeks. Milan catwalks offer the most established, legendary Italian fashion houses, including Armani and Cavalli. Their fashion week is commercially the most important for menswear because of the popularity of Italian fashion, from casual to elegant. Paris, on the other hand, is creative, established and the most influential of all the menswear shows. Paris shows are the perfect combination of creativity, heritage and commerciality. In menswear trend research all of the major presentations need to be reviewed and analysed.

5.19
Fashion catwalks offer valuable information in trend forecasting, often used for close-to-season analysis. The runaway is also good moment to confirm a previously made forecast, as done here by Fashion Snoops for spring/summer 2017.

5.20

Trade Shows

There are two types of trade show that dictate the trend calendar: those where designers buy raw materials and those where designers sell their designs to shops and retailers (usually about six months after the raw material shows). As a trend forecaster, you need to keep abreast of all these events. When you attend retail-geared trade shows, your work will be more analytical because you are viewing next season's product. Numerous trade shows take place globally with much of the information from these shows being made available online (modemonline.com). The raw material shows will also present many material companies, such as Material ConneXion, which will have a stand or a presentation area inside the events. Also, many trend agencies and trend book manufacturers will have stands to sell their trend books and services. Trade shows are a must for menswear trend forecasting.

FASHION: STREET STYLE

Street style photography is becoming increasingly influential and has exploded in the media, especially after Scott Schuman reintroduced the idea in the digital age. Trend agencies and even printed media are mainly interested in people who are in the menswear week circuit, either before or after the show. The men of various events are today often well covered, including music festivals and art shows. However, the most important street style event is Pitti Uomo. It takes place bi-annually in Florence, Italy. Street style has become an important part of fashion communication. It is democratic, creating an opportunity for any man to express himself. Everyone can have a chance at being a menswear trendsetter.

5.20
Pitti Uomo is an important event for seasonal styling inspiration.

TRADE SHOW BASICS

The time frames for trend forecasting differ depending on the client or the purpose. The two main trade shows to cover are the material shows and the finished product shows. When covering a show as a trend professional, make sure to register as a professional, preferably with press accreditations and permissions to photograph. Many shows are quite strict with press permissions and want to see proof in a form of publication or some type of Internet presence. When entering a trade show as a student, check with the show organizers which days allow student entry. Trade shows usually limit student entry to the last day or two of the show.

Entering the show as a student can be very intimidating. Most vendors are there to do business and want to focus on revenue generating encounters, but some can be also welcoming to students. Make it clear immediately that you are a student and would like to have a look at the items at the stand, and request permission to take photos. Visiting trade shows is an essential part of a student's real-life business experience.

When deciding on which trade shows to cover, for future seasons' trend work the raw material shows are a good starting point. The material shows are also a good opportunity to verify the trend direction. The three essential types of materials trade shows are: knit and yarn; textiles,

suiting and shirting fabrics; and leather. These material shows all take place weeks apart. They should be visited bi-annually to have a good clear foundation as to what materials are on offer. Most trade shows offer trend lectures and seminars, which are also a good source of information and may establish the mood of the overall direction of the show.

Material sourcing shows are an essential part of trend research for menswear and provide an opportunity to start establishing relationships and networking with the manufacturers. Sometimes clients want trend professionals to help with sourcing as well. Because these shows are professional, it is important to get accreditation from the show organizers beforehand. The press office usually provides press passes to trend professionals from agencies and sometimes to freelancers.

There are some basic rules for visiting trade shows and the stands. As you enter each booth, you should advise the trade show exhibitor as to the purpose of your visit. Some trade shows are very strict with photography (for obvious reasons), so it is always necessary to ask permission from the exhibitor.

5.21

5.22

TYPES OF MATERIAL TRADE SHOWS

Material shows are important for trend forecasting, since this is the first opportunity to see what materials may end up in the finished garments. There are very strong signals already present in materials shows that provide an indication of what the future trends may be. There are no specific menswear materials trade shows, but shows such as Milano Unica and Première Vision Paris are popular textile shows for menswear professionals. Pitti Filati (which takes place in Florence, Italy) is a leading yarn show for the knitwear industry. Pitti Filati boasts a trend area that showcases knit innovations for the future. The leading leather trade show is Linea Pelle, which takes place twice a year in Milan. The raw materials shows each have their own trend area. They often provide trend presentations that are attended by visitors and manufacturers alike. This also makes it a good opportunity to validate your culture-based trend research and start further development of your work.

Materials shows have several categories and areas to show – the trend area, which is a prominent area of materials from exhibitors, being the most interesting for many because it is where you usually see the latest material developments. The areas in each show can include yarn, textile, leather, synthetics, accessories, design services, finished product manufacturing services and denim areas, to name a few. The raw materials shows are for manufacturing a product, which means that they take place about six months before brands show their product in the finished product trade shows. These in turn occur about six months before the finished goods are in shops (i.e., the relevant material trade shows take place about one year before the retailer season).

Trend research has to start even earlier, especially if the raw materials market is the client. If a brand subscribes to the service, trend research can start along with the raw materials show. If a retailer is subscribing to the service, it would usually be for a mixture of analysis and forecasting. Retailers often use trend information as a buying guide and for merchandising direction.

Knit and Yarn

Pitti Filati in Florence, Italy is one of the first tradeshows that gives an indication of directions in colour and material – for knit and yarn in particular. The show takes place one year before the retail finished product. Pitti Filati also has a trend area that offers suggestions and culture-based trends for the upcoming season. The show is organized in one central space in Fortezza da Basso, Florence, Italy.

The most important area of the show is the trend area or 'Spacio Ricerca', designed and organized by Angelo Figus and Nicole Miller. The area is well curated, and each visitor receives a yarn-covered colour card based on the presented trend stories. It is important to read the accompanying text, which explains the emotional and cultural foundation of the trends. Another key space for new innovation and research is the Fashion at Work area, where many designers present new yarn and knit innovations.

The Pitti Filati show is essential to understanding the signals for colour and knit. It is one of the first opportunities to understand the directions colour will go during the coming year in knitwear and fashion in general.

Textiles, Shirting and Suiting

Milano Unica and Première Vision Paris are important trade shows for menswear materials. Unica is a leading Italian textile show known for men's high-level shirting material. Here purchases are made for manufacturing, collection sampling and collection making. The show takes place in the city centre fair and has recently gained popularity due to the increased interest in menswear. Often standing room only, the trend presentation is a must for many companies that need to understand the direction of textiles for the upcoming season. Milano Unica also has a Shanghai China edition to cater to this important market. Première Vision (PV), Paris, is a leader in across-the-board material trade fairs. Paris is traditionally the centre of fashion, and it caters to its reputation with 'best of the best' displays in this trade fair. The show boasts impressive halls displaying everything from denim to shirting and leather. Most fashion companies go to these fairs and most stands base their offer on trends. Some stands first present viewers with the trend mood boards before allowing them to advance to the material collections. Première Vision has also editions in New York, Sao Paolo and Shanghai.

5.23

5.21
The Pitti Filati trend area is a go-to for new directions in yarns and knit design options.

5.22
It is good practice to create a brief materials summary after each trade show. This will help to focus on the essentials of the season as well as provide a more personal, non-digital approach.

5.23
Première Vision is an essential trade show to attend for fabric sourcing and trends.

Leather and Synthetics Trade Shows

Linea Pelle is the world's leading leather, accessories, components, synthetics and textiles fair, and it takes place in Milan, Italy. This show is visited by manufacturers of footwear, accessories and clothes, whether leather or imitation leather. The show is very much based on trends, with trend lectures and a welcoming trend area at the entrance of the show. Visitors to the leather show should first go to this 'trend area' to see material, trimmings, outsoles and hardware categorized under various trends. Linea Pelle also does trade events in New York and London, offering other opportunities to cover the raw material aspect of menswear when travel to Italy is not possible. Material shows, such as Linea Pelle, also offer colour and trend information for sale in book or digital format. The material shows do not generally separate the colour and material stories into menswear or womenswear, but provide a base for you to construct your own story. Some stories will appear more suitable to one or the other. Raw materials shows are very important because they are the foundation of the seasons to come.

5.24
Linea Pelle is a leading leather show in Milan offering various leather and synthetic options for apparel, footwear, accessories and interiors.

5.24

FINISHED PRODUCT TRADE SHOWS

The materials trade shows are followed by the finished product / fashion trade shows. These shows are an opportunity for the sample garment to be presented to buyers. They take place about six months after the raw materials shows. The design houses normally buy the material from the raw materials shows to make the final garment. Trend forecasters follow the schedule of these shows because this is where the new garments are presented (along with the catwalk shows).

One opportunity to see new season finished garments is the London Collections Men (LCM) show in London. LCM is forward thinking, young and often considered the most trend-setting of the shows. Around the same time is the Pitti Uomo show in Florence, Italy. This show has product at all levels of the industry, focusing on the commercial (but especially on high-end and Made in Italy products). Paris is another important venue for previewing the next season. During Paris there are many trade shows that are operating at same time as the menswear catwalks shows. In Paris Tranoï Homme and MAN are the most important. Industry-specific fashion and trade show research is essential to be able to provide valuable information on trends.

Trade shows such as Project, Capsule and Tranoï Homme place their exhibitions to coincide with the fashion catwalks and the buyers' arrival in town. However, menswear continues to be presented after the official menswear buying season. This is because many buyers might only do one trip to a show, which means the menswear labels often do not only focus on one show, but rather attempt to cover as many selling opportunities as possible. The main buying opportunities occur during the menswear season, but today buyers are becoming less likely to place orders at one show only. Buyers can view product across the whole season. For example, the new season shoes can be presented in Pitti Uomo in June and again in Micam or Las Vegas at the end of August – almost three months later.

As a trend forecaster, it is not only important to see what is on offer in these shows, but also to understand how buying works. The buying for menswear is concentrated in two seasons: spring/summer and fall/winter. Spring/summer kicks off in early June, with London menswear shows buying for the following spring, and it ends with Paris menswear at the end of June. For fall/winter, the same order happens, with the first shows starting usually in the second week of January (buying for the following fall) and ending again with Paris at the end of January. The trade shows vary greatly between cities, which is the reason to visit all of them in order to gain a better understanding for your trend focus. For example, Pitti Uomo is very different from ISPO – which specializes in sportswear from performance to leisure.

MODEMONLINE

5.25
Navigating the fashion calendar at the same time as the trade show and materials calendar is complex task. As a trend professional you will be working in synchronization with all of them. Modem Online (http://www .modemonline.com /fashion/) offers the best and most comprehensive calendar information.

5.26
It is good practice to keep a pen and sketch book at hand to draw ideas. These can often prove more valuable than taking photos.

5.27
Trend should be the connecting point of all the various areas of your research.

June 2016	July 2016	August 2016	September 2016	October 2016
London men's London Collections: Men from Friday 10 June to Monday 13 June shows & presentations press multi-label showrooms designer showrooms tradeshows events	**Paris** Couture & Haute Couture fall-winter 16 / 17 from Sunday 03 July to Thursday 07 July shows & presentations press events	**Munich** SS 17 Market Week from Saturday 06 Aug. to Tuesday 09 Aug. multi-label showrooms designer showrooms tradeshows	**New York** women's New York Fashion Week Women's from Wed. 07 Sept. to Thursday 15 Sept. shows & presentations press multi-label showrooms designer showrooms tradeshows events	**Dubai** Arab Fashion Week from Thursday 06 Oct. to Monday 10 Oct.
Florence men's from Tuesday 14 June to Friday 17 June shows & presentations press multi-label showrooms designer showrooms tradeshows events	**New York** men's New York Fashion Week Men's from Monday 11 July to Thursday 14 July shows & presentations press multi-label showrooms designer showrooms tradeshows events	**Copenhagen** from Wed. 10 Aug. to Friday 12 Aug. shows & presentations press multi-label showrooms designer showrooms tradeshows events	**London** women's from Friday 16 Sept. to Tuesday 20 Sept. tradeshows	**Shanghai** Shanghai Fashion Week from Wed. 12 Oct. to Thursday 20 Oct. tradeshows
Milan men's from Saturday 18 June to Tuesday 21 June shows & presentations press multi-label showrooms designer showrooms tradeshows events	**Miami** FUNKSHION: Fashion Week Miami Beach from Wed. 13 July to Tuesday 19 July tradeshows	**Las Vegas** SS 17 Market Week from Sunday 14 Aug. to Wed. 17 Aug. multi-label showrooms designer showrooms tradeshows	**Milan** women's from Wed. 21 Sept. to Tuesday 27 Sept. shows & presentations multi-label showrooms designer showrooms tradeshows	**Los Angeles** SS 17 Market Week from Monday 17 Oct. to Wed. 19 Oct. tradeshows
Paris men's from Wed. 22 June to Sunday 26 June	**Düsseldorf** SS 17 Market Week from Friday 22 July to Thursday 28 July multi-label showrooms designer showrooms	**Stockholm** from Monday 29 Aug. to Wed. 31 Aug. shows & presentations press	**Paris** women's from Tuesday 27 Sept. to Wed. 05 Oct. press multi-label showrooms designer showrooms tradeshows events	**Seoul** Hera Seoul Fashion Week from Monday 17 Oct. to Saturday 22 Oct. tradeshows
				Tokyo Amazon Fashion Week Tokyo from Monday 17 Oct. to Sunday 23 Oct. multi-label showrooms designer showrooms tradeshows

5.25

TRADE SHOW SUMMARY

Trade shows provide good signposts for the trend research cycle, whether for forecasting or analysis. The work is multifaceted because there is a need for early analysis and also information gathering for clients that represent magazines, buyers and brands. This is why it is better to focus on gathering information (images, literature, samples) and work out the directions later. With the trade show information in hand, you have a good moment to validate your work so far.

Naturally, it is impossible to cover all the shows, but it is important to have first-hand experience, witnessing how the business works from the inside. For ones you cannot attend, descriptions may appear in various blogs and organizer websites – although this information might be available too late. Remember, shows are only accessible to fashion professionals, so appropriate advance accreditation is needed. Once information from trade shows has been gathered, it is often quite clear what the trends are. The trends that you sense through your observation at the shows may not necessarily coincide with those the show organizers suggest. What you can do is to summarize the information in a way that serves your personal trend vision (or a combination of personal and trade show vision) for a corporate client.

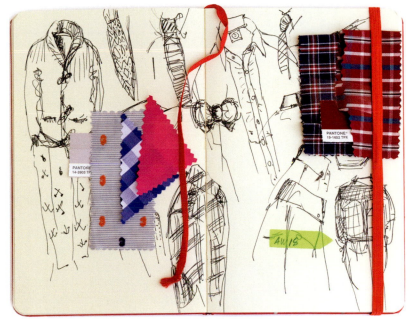

5.26

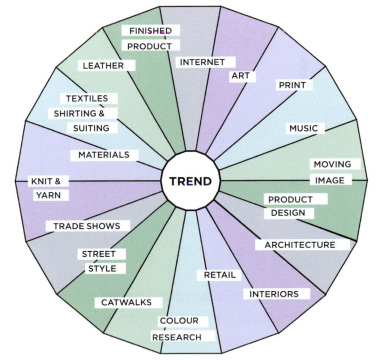

5.27

ORGANIZING YOUR RESEARCH

Everybody has his or her own way of categorizing information, whether it is material in digital format or pinning magazine tears on a foam board. The important part of the analytical process is to start looking at the connecting points to start the creative pooling of ideas. One method is to use traditional techniques of brainstorming (writing a list of all ideas as they occur) or mind-mapping (writing or drawing what comes to mind and connecting the words and images with circles and lines). Try to discover the key points and evidence from all the research. If you have been researching art and have visited numerous art shows, what were the main media used and what styles, topics or ideas were included? What are the topical issues of the moment? Are there materials in the raw materials shows that reflect this mood? Are there visual representations in the catwalk shows that can bring the trends closer to the commercial opportunity? By writing down key words and key concepts or even slogans you will be able to expand your research.

After creating a clear list of key words, search the Internet to see if there are some current developments in the given subject. Perhaps an outstanding theme in an art show was using ready-made or found objects (such as an exhibition at London's Barbican called 'Artist as a Collector'). This could lead you to research some other artist (such as Theaster Gates) to understand more what this type of art is all about. All the factual and data collecting forms a foundation for becoming a credible trend forecaster.

TREND SENSE EXERCISE

In this qualitative exercise, you will teach yourself to be completely aware and learn not only to look, but to fully sense the world around you. With this observational technique you can learn a lot that you would normally not notice.

Select a space or place that fits your research. For example, choose a public square if researching general menswear usage. Choose a train station or airport if information on travel habits is needed. Even a gym or hospital could make for interesting observation. (Consider privacy laws and etiquette.)

Record a general overview of the space and its occupants, including a visual account with details of sounds and even smell or taste. Also explore the tactility of the space. What is the demographic of the space? Are the people you see tourists, families or business people? After the overall mood and atmosphere is decided, start focusing your observation on the other aspects of the space. Visual imagery is obviously important, so taking pictures is encouraged. The image can be a still image or a moving image; the most powerful image created is the mental image. Record the sound of the space.

Storytelling is a big part of a trend professional's job. You are not only delivering factual information but also inspiring people. By recording the sound of the space you are occupying as well as its sights, you can play back sounds that will take you mentally back to this space to find interesting nuances from it. Every city and neighbourhood has a sound.

We need to engage more deeply with our environment and understand where we are from and where we exist. We live at work, where increasingly work and learning is done in a virtual space. If you bring the primary experience to the clients alongside the regular trends information, you will have added more value to your product.

The exercise result can be used as a field study example or as a foundation for larger primary research or a presentation. Your audience will always be impressed when field study level information is used.

PETER BETSCHE
CEO Arvenco

Peter Betsche is a CEO of Swiss company Arvenco. His company sources and develops garments for various global brands in Asia. He has over twenty years of experience in textile industries and has worked with international brands such as Hugo Boss and Tiger of Sweden.

5.28

How do menswear textile and materials differ from womenswear? If we would ask a woman to place three words in order of importance – she would most probably classify them in the following sequence: Look > Price > Comfort.

The female consumer of today would like to have more natural fibres than are offered by brands. Many feel that they are forced to buy synthetic garments – but if the look is right, the women still buy! Since natural fibres such as silk, cotton, cashmere are expensive and resources limited, synthetics are here to match the features and to make the garment more affordable.

Female wardrobe turn-around time is faster than men's, yet the industry budgets have to be tighter to be able to offer fashions at reasonable pricing. Women's clothes manufacturing has a much lower standard of manufacturing in general than men's. I even know of a few brands (preferring superior quality) who produce female shirts and blouses in men's shirting lines!

Classically a man sets his priority more on the Comfort > Price > Look formula. Men tend to buy less than women do, so they do not mind investing in clothing and good quality as comfort. Men are more loyal to a brand and will repeat buy, based on comfort level. Therefore, natural fibres are a main consideration for purchase, reflecting that it is the 'real thing' and not something fake and superficial.

What are the most important trade shows for menswear materials? The most important fabric show is definitely Première Vision, held in Paris twice a year (February/September). It is an international show, which attracts visitors from all over the world to this glamorous city. Munich Fabric Start has gained popularity recently in the fabric show circuit. Visitors are mainly from German-speaking countries (Germany, Austria and Switzerland), but it attracts more and more international visitors. Its counterpart is Italy's Milano Unica – a regrouping of the small traditional Italian fairs, such as Moda In, Prato Expo, Idea Biella etc. Visitors are mainly from Italy and Spain, but also have strong representation from other international regions.

The largest fabric show in the world is definitely Shanghai Tex – organized by Messe Frankfurt twice a year in Shanghai. Unfortunately the show is very late in the sourcing calendar – so it is used by the buyers to re-cap existing developments or orders. Sometimes the show is used to place some new orders or to look for new industry partners.

5.28
Peter Betsche specializes in garment development for international brands in Asia.

5.29

Techtextil is an innovation material fair held bi-annually. The fair has interesting new finishes, raw materials and functions. It is a fair that is appreciated by sportswear, especially performance wear and technical textiles companies. Smart textiles are often shown here for the first time, making this a good show for future trends.

What are the main fabric menswear trends of the moment? In general fabrication turns more quiet and back to solids. We are not yet back to the solid boom of the mid-1990s, since in menswear micro fabric designs are still important. However, the print boom of the last few years is getting slower. Brushed and super soft qualities are growing in importance. In the yarn-dyed segment the use of Mouliné yarns might be seen more frequently and the melange yarns are still relevant. Fibre-wise, these are wool blends in the winter – and warp knitted shirts, reminiscent of the 1970s, but with the comfort of modern times.

When considering trend direction for fabrics – how long will it take to develop samples in general? Fabric development has become more a continuous process rather than seasonal. Mills are continuously developing new product– depending naturally on the segment. When the world's fabric industry is showing a season in retail a year from now, the sportswear companies are already working on a season ahead of that. But from a design idea – over to a CAD – then to a hand loom – to finally end up with a sample run weaving – it might technically last one month, but practically will take two months or even more to develop.

5.29
Munich Fabric Start has started to have more international visitors; it offers various materials to the apparel business.

5.30

What are the latest sustainability trends? The main trend is the transparency trend – whether it's about the composition of the product or the setup and organization of a company. An innovative player in this regard is Switcher, who wants the end customer to be responsible and compensate for the CO_2 emission of the product bought. They also want to be able to have traceability of the product and total production cycle of a specific product. There are other interesting projects and initiatives such as 'cradle to cradle' production and companies such as Bluesign – all aiming for more sustainable production.

How long are the cycles of trends usually? Any examples? From birth to death, a trend might last as long as seven years. It is the same life span a fabric product has. The trend is on its peak for one season as innovation and novelty, and it takes a further one to two seasons to become more widely adopted. However, fabric and design trends are at risk in that they are often too early. It is important to remember that to commercialize a trend takes two to three seasons. If trends don't survive this long, the colours and weaves might be adjusted to help the longevity.

What is the biggest recent change in menswear fabrication? The fashion industry is continuously thinking of ways to better understand men's minds and to figure out how to make them more interested in updating the wardrobe more frequently. In my opinion men are more interested in things of a technical nature, sparking this interest in technical fabrications. Smart textiles used in casual or sportswear or intelligent textiles that increase performance has been a big change, items that raise the comfort level of men.

What are some exciting new men's fabrics? There are many – and all the time new ones. For example, coffee fabric fibres made from coffee grounds waste have been developed. One of the big benefits is the anti-odour qualities of this new textile. Another new fabric researched is one that increases the heat and blood circulation, which in turn increases the level of blood oxygen and performance

5.30
Arvenco sources and develops garments for various global brands in Asia.

5.31
Natural fibres are increasingly important for men when buying shirts.

5.32
Fabric development has become more a continuous process rather than seasonal one, states Peter Betsche.

in performance sports. There are also developments in energy harvesting with possibilities of fabric that could charge your phone. Whether it's the fabrication of breathable yet water repellent, UV protective or the Nike project of a transparent shoe, new innovation opportunities are plenty.

What is the future of menswear fabrication? Is it growing? There is a future of men's fashion. The interest for fashion has lately been growing rapidly and becomes more important in emerging countries such as eastern Europe and China, as well. Man has become more interested in his appearance. One big issue is population control. How can we make fibres with a world growing population? Just recently, the Polytechnical University of Zürich presented the first knitwear manufactured with fibres made of offal from slaughterhouses.

But the largest growth and challenge will be for our ageing generation. We are the first fashion generation to get older with the history of fashion consumerism. This means the future of menswear will need to be as functional as work-wear uniforms. I imagine myself eating my spaghetti in an old folks home and still being able to drink coffee with my friends, without worrying about the tomato sauce stains on my white shirt.

5.31

5.32

CHAPTER SUMMARY

As in any creative field, research is possibly the most important part of the trend work process. In this chapter we discussed how well-conducted research provides a credible foundation for the forecast or analysis. This will add value to your analysis and prediction. The initial decision that determines the starting point of your research is whether you are analyzing the trends of the season or predicting something more long term.

The first part of the process of research is gathering information, which can mean a variety of things: using the Internet, viewing art, reading books, listening to music and attending concerts, watching films, looking at interior design and architecture, shopping retail stores, and finding out more about colour. All this is in addition to analyzing the catwalks, street style, and the many trade shows.

A trend forecaster is a sponge with the ability to absorb information from everything in the surroundings. Curiosity is a key characteristic of a forecaster. When researching menswear trends, it is important to keep an eye open to information that is not limited to menswear. Anything and everything can be an early signal to trends. After the broader view is observed, more focused research can be conducted.

HOMEWORK ASSIGNMENTS

1. Have a look at various trade shows in portals such as modemonline.com to see how trade shows overlap. What seasonal order can you detect from the calendar?
2. What are the top five cultural movements at the moment? Which ones do you think will affect menswear – and how?
3. Which are the most influential menswear retailers in your area? What brands do they stock?

DISCUSSION ACTIVITIES AND PROJECTS

1. Practice street photography with fellow students to understand the importance of light and focus. Take full body shots and detail shots. Analyse in class.
2. Select the top five topics that are in media at the moment. Go to the library and look for images that relate to these topics.
3. Look up the trade shows and events mentioned in this chapter. See what trends were apparent in the recent shows and discuss how they may translate to menswear.
4. What is the difference between primary and secondary research?

KEY WORDS

primary research
qualitative
quantitative
secondary research
trade shows

6.1

6.1
Trend presentation
is when gathered
data becomes
a workable
product. This
image represents
a trend that has
been influenced
by a resurgence of
historic inspired
interiors and the
new romantic
nuances of Gucci's
creative director
Alessandro Michele.

Application of Trend Data

LEARNING OBJECTIVES

- Apply trend data.
- Recognize different types of trend customers.
- Differentiate various levels of trend service.
- Analyse and forecast colour trends.
- Create an inspiring trend forecast.
- Conduct a trend workshop.

INTRODUCTION

Trends and trend research are useful in several different areas of the men's fashion business. Within larger menswear corporations there are often specific menswear brands that utilize trend information in various different ways, from packaging to selection of materials. Similarly, retailers use numerous sectors, such as general trend direction, colour and material information, to influence their decision process from visual merchandising to buying.

The manufacturing world can be divided into two main sectors: the textile and material producers, and the manufacturers of goods. The textile and material producers are mainly interested in colour and colour forecasting, but also consider other sectors of trends, such as mood and feel and surface design. Another influential part of the industry are trade shows. There are only a few trade shows dedicated to menswear, yet most of the shows do have menswear well represented. The trade shows vary from materials, manufacturing and sourcing shows to finished product shows.

Finally, trend information is something that can be useful and beneficial to the consumer through publications, mainly in the form of advice on what to wear and what to buy, as well as styling advice. Consumers are exposed to trend information through various media channels, from menswear fashion magazines to online sources.

Trend deliverables are an important part of a trend forecaster's world and in this chapter we explore how to create an effective report as well as how to conduct a trend workshop. The scope is very large as to how the information may be used, but the starting point – the trend itself – will always be the same.

Avant guardian

An astute selection of small scale, intricate designs, worn in abundance, takes its cue from the inspiration of cravat and foulard effects. Here, even the plains are patterned. Tapestry effects, engraved jacquards, micro dobbies and mini geometrics proliferate for a new neatly proportioned but easy sports layered style. Assured, forward looking, and confident in your own future!

6.2

6.2
Trend information can be used in various ways. Here, textile direction appears from *Textile View* magazine, where the actual material swatches are incorporated into the illustrated story.

TRENDS IN THE CORPORATE WORLD

Most larger menswear companies use online trend services. Online channels provide a wealth of information for companies that give them an insight into today's market. Online trend services, such as WGSN and Trendstop, are membership-paid services. They can be costly for the average consumer, but are very valuable for companies. Some fashion colleges subscribe to trend agency services, providing students with a valuable source of information. The online services offer information that can be a powerful tool for any menswear business. The agencies will cover areas such as trade shows, retail in-store and catwalk reviews. In addition, the actual trends and trend forecasts are featured in various formats that can be in printed form, digital, film or online webinars, which, with today's technology, are becoming more popular.

A large reason that online services are so popular for menswear businesses is that all the information is easily accessible. The most important information can be gathered when visiting stores and trade shows oneself, but it is almost impossible to visit every single store and show in person. Therefore, web portals provide an invaluable overview of retail and what is happening in the global marketplace by allowing companies to view all the important shows and see the highlights without personally being there. Trade shows provide information that helps menswear buyers to confirm their strategies for the season to come or to help plan future purchases. The visual merchandising team can also gain ideas for dressing the shop floor or windows from various inspirational material often offered by these websites. The amount of information from trend portals can be overwhelming; the workshop exercise at the end of this chapter will help you to translate trend information into practical terms.

6.3
Trend presentations and workshops help you to bring trend information closer to the end user.

6.4
Before setting out to work on the trend deliverables, it is essential to know who your audience is. For example, Zara as a company would be interested in all the latest catwalk information.

UNDERSTANDING YOUR AUDIENCE

In order to prepare an effective trend presentation, an understanding of the intended audience is essential. The direction of the presentation will depend on whether it is for a manufacturer, a brand, a retailer or an end consumer (e.g., a printed or online publication). As a trend forecaster you would most likely work with all these various sectors of the industry. The delivery will be different for each of these sectors because of the timing required. Before going forward with any project, you would need to clarify from your target (client) exactly who will be using the information, in order to get a full understanding of what is needed from you. Expectations can vary, and it is important to come to a full agreement, especially if contracts are drawn up. Sometimes companies are not sure how to use trend information, so this is also a good opportunity to educate and create a customized package that offers the best possible results. This will also help with pricing your service. Before asking more specific questions, you would need to fully research the company – understand exactly what they do and how they do it – from pricing and distribution to communication.

6.3

6.4

EXERCISE

Research a mainstream fashion company online in order to get a better understanding of who they are. Look at key factors such as price points, distribution, competition, strengths and, above all, weaknesses. Determine where, in your opinion, the company needs the most help and come up with a strategy.

CLIENT ASSESSMENT

The main sectors of the menswear business that use trend information are brands, retail, manufacturing, trade show organizers and publications. When researching the client needs, it is good to have a set of specific questions relating to each of these industries to help better determine how the information will be used. Again, the trend starting point will be the same, but eventually it will be geared towards the specific user needs. Your deliverables will greatly depend on this research, which will determine the time used on the project and ultimately will decide the costing.

Brand

When assessing brand needs, you need to determine whether it will be the fashion design or the marketing team that will predominantly use your information. If working with designers, do they only need inspiration and references to help with their design process, or do they want you to be involved at a deeper level? Sometimes brands want help in translating trends to material language, while helping with the actual sourcing of materials. If such design and collection development is needed, it would add a substantial amount of work to the order – another consideration when costing your product.

Retail

Retail encompasses a large part of fashion (see Chapter 3). However, when assessing retail as the end user, you need to consider the actual section using the information. In other words, your presentation can address the buyers, the visual merchandising or even the communication team. Your presentation can be something that covers bigger themes and the overall direction of retail. It can be as inspirational as a colour direction, as broad as what is happening globally in retail, or as specific as close-to-season analysis. The important part is that you study your subject well and offer something that matches the retail level the client occupies.

6.5

Manufacturing

If working with a raw materials developer, it is important to ascertain whether they are interested in material innovation research, colour trend development, or on-trend trade show communication. Producers of materials such as yarn, textile and leather will need trend information (on average) two years before the planned end product retail date. Material producers (such as a tannery or a mill) are very interested in colour, but have become more interested in cultural factors that influence the consumer. The brand they sell to is their end customer, so in this instance it would be essential to investigate the brands that will be buying from the manufacturer. If the client is a brand, their typical consumer details are key. The most important question to ask is whether the brand wants to reach a new type of client or just reinforce the current client base. In addition to this, other areas to discuss are what type of brand or customer buys the product: Are they young or more mature? Is the brand sporty, casual, classic or luxury level? You can also ask what are the strengths, weaknesses, opportunities and threats (known as SWOT analysis) of the brand that will use the manufacturer information.

6.5
Brands such as John Smedley place great importance and focus on colour in their collection planning.

Trade Shows

Working with trade shows entails helping the show organizer to research that season's trends (within the trade show exhibitions) and exploring how that can inspire the attendee. The trend area (usually a specific zone within the trade show) presents various trends to help the attendee with the buying process. For the trend consultant, what this often entails is collecting current information from the show exhibitors in order to gather a selection of actual items to curate a trend area. For example, Linea Pelle has a special section with tables that consist of collected materials from various vendors. The footwear and apparel shows can have a static installation or a catwalk to present a trend direction at the trade show.

Publications

Publications use trend information often and are closest to the end consumer. If working on a trend or editorial piece for a magazine, it is important to learn about their readers. Again, the trend-based information needed may vary greatly between commercial magazines, department store catalogues and more forward-thinking men's publications. Magazines such as *View* and *Zoom on Fashion Trends* have forecasting editorials in them, while more commercial magazines would have more seasonal analytical editorials. The better you know the target audience of the magazine, the better the service you can provide.

6.6
Textile View magazine has a very strong understanding of their end user, which is the fashion trade.

6.6

Service Level

After assessing the type of client and the specific area of the company receiving your trend report, you can begin to determine what level of service you can offer. If the company is interested in a full package, it will involve following trend development and application throughout the whole process, from the first meeting to the end of product development. This requires the most commitment from the client and may require a partnership of close to a year at a time. They may incorporate this information into their own relevant research, in order to create a type of brand guideline for the season. The levels of service that can be offered may vary depending on the size and capabilities of the provider. For example, a seasonal colour, material or catwalk analysis could be done by an individual, such as a freelancer; however, a bigger project that involves more resources – for example, sample development – would need a larger team. The most common commission is a seasonal trend update that would require a single presentation. Other levels may include closer follow-up of the project, or a fully immersed trend delivery.

After the initial client assessment, start thinking of the focus of the presentation, determining if the project is to cover a full menswear collection or part of it. For example, is the main focus apparel, footwear, or a mix of the two? If working with a retailer, is the focus a specific buying group, or a particular area of visual merchandising? Other things to determine are whether the client wants a general 'mood' presentation or needs a more specific and detailed working presentation. Working with a material producer is often less complicated than working with a brand or retailer because sample direction and buying plans are really not needed. Material producers usually specialize in one area, such as yarn production, textiles or leather.

TREND DELIVERABLES

A trend presentation can be digital or printed, can contain material references or actual material swatches or can involve all of these things. As an example, a full format corporate presentation would include a digital presentation, along with printed documents and colour and material swatches. Producing a solely digital presentation is far less expensive in comparison to a printed forecast with material swatches.

Sourcing materials can be a time-consuming and sometimes overwhelming task, but has added value for most clients because of their time and cost savings. Often larger fashion companies have someone who specializes in material sourcing. Alternatively, a simple materials reference board may be presented that represents the material world as discussed, using colour coding systems, such as Pantone chips. In practice it is virtually impossible to show exact colours unless the material to be used is exactly dyed to match the colour coding system.

HOW TO CREATE A TREND PRESENTATION

The following sections provide some basic elements to give you a framework on how to construct a trend forecast. Although these can be used as a basis for your project, it will be beneficial to develop your own signature style. The three-point theory is a simple formula to use before fleshing out your distinct style.

With these three points, you will take something that is not tangible (point 1) to something that is tangible (point 3) with a phase of the process we call the bridge (point 2). The three points are only to be used as a roadmap, with each section consisting of several pages. Also, within the presentation you will have a colour and materials section, with any material that can help with the presentation. The three points will give you a good framework on which to build your presentation.

You can start the presentation from a cultural starting point (CSP), bridging it to a product to fit your audience: CSP–BRIDGE–PRODUCT. The bridge is to show how the more intangible notion of sociocultural factors become more tangible factors – ultimately, the product, whatever that may be. The bridge is the verification stage or the manifestation of trend as early signals in the marketplace. The product suggestion can be many things, but here we will focus on menswear apparel and accessories.

For example, if the trend is the 1980s, you would show in the CSP part of your presentation films, interiors and exhibitions that have triggered this trend. In the bridge section you can show early products from directional brands, street styling mixed with images from maybe furniture or product design that is affirming the trend (make sure to use contemporary visuals from current shows and exhibitions). In the product part you would illustrate how the client should use the trend. If you are presenting to a brand, you would draw sample items showing how the brand can use the trend in their product.

6.7
The value of your service depends on the time spent on it. Determine early in the process if detailed design work is needed or if only 'direction pointing' illustrations are required.

Another area to consider is your audience and the formats they require. There are various free options for developing a presentation, but the ones that require online connectivity are to be avoided, unless there is an absolute guarantee of perfect connectivity on the day of your presentation. There is nothing worse than having a presentation that does not work in front of an audience. Always test your presentation and save a PDF backup, in case the original format does not work. Always be prepared to have a back-up plan if technology fails.

When making a trends presentation you would ideally create each slide independently, outside the presentation format. If high definition images are used, one slide can sometimes become too large for PowerPoint or Keynote to handle. Work the slides in InDesign (preferred) or in Photoshop. These are basic skills to be mastered in order to create a visually interesting story and a powerful presentation. Some basic layout skills are also needed when preparing a presentation, including font and colour considerations. The rule is to have the images speak for themselves, rather than allowing graphic elements to disrupt your story. Spinning visuals and sound effects are to be avoided, especially if presenting to a corporate or public audience, such as a trade show audience.

One important thing to remember regarding presenting images that are not your own: copyright. In a closed, private presentation you may not need permission from a copyright holder (check the law and compare it to how you're using the image), but in a public setting, especially if published/printed images will be provided, the permission of the copyright holder must be obtained.

6.8
The cultural starting point clearly provides an impression of what the trend direction will be.

CULTURAL STARTING POINT

In Chapter 4 we discussed various ways to detect a trend. In practical terms this means looking for visuals and images that best express the trend. In fashion this is called a mood board and is used to assist with the design process. However, in trend presentation the mood opener is a starting point that sets the mood for the presentation and helps to make the case. The mood opener can be a single image or a group of images. The opening page with images is very important because it provides a first impression of what is to come. In digital format the image references will serve mainly as a backdrop to help with your storytelling, but they need to be strong enough to be viewed on their own and without explanation. It is also useful to include a slide or a page that summarizes the trend starting point in a few sentences. Sometimes it is possible to start the presentation with the summary and then move on to the images.

6.8

THE BRIDGE

The bridge connects the socioeconomic and cultural points to a more concrete realm of products. After you have determined the starting point for your trend, start thinking of how to connect it to your audience (i.e., the bridge). For example, if you want to connect it to footwear, start looking at the trend and how it could connect to the world of footwear. In this section you can start mixing trend images with actual product images. You can also combine art with product, or interiors with product and footwear. The 'bridge' will help the audience to understand the translation of the trend to a product opportunity. Look for visuals that match the trend starting point with product atmospheres. For example, if your trend starting point has something to do with modernism and contemporary architecture, your bridge should also reflect this.

TREND INTRO

Look at some of the trends that you have detected and write an introduction of a few sentences to capture the mood of the trend. In the starting point, you can reference anything that led you to the trend: news, media, exhibitions or any other early signal information.

THE PRODUCT

This is the product translation part of your trend presentation. If you have the previously mentioned contemporary aesthetic as a starting point, your end product should clearly reflect that. The menswear product examples should be from forward thinking, early adopter concepts, whether retail, catwalks or street. This will provide clear directions for design teams and/or buyers.

TREND PROFILE

Profiling is about the personification of the trend. In other words, who is the person that will most likely fit the trend profile? If the trend is about seaside living, the person you would visualize would not be a city slicker wearing a suit. The visuals that support the person you have in mind can be from fashion editorials or street styling. When planning advertising strategy, a look-book or general communication for the season, tying it to the trend makes more sense.

COLOUR

Colour is the most important part of the trend forecast because it is the most difficult area for many companies to understand. Colour translation of the trend is complicated since colour will only be 'true' when the product is made. When you suggest a colour palette, it is good to have matching materials ready, making the visualization of the product easier. However, the starting point is first to make the colour palette, then find matching materials or product sample images. Colour is also one of the best ways to link the early trend signals to a concrete concept. Many companies focus on colour, creating colour stories that make sense for their collections. With colour you would create a main colour palette from an image that is the colour amalgamation of the trend. Finding the images can be challenging, but this is why it is essential to have an extensive

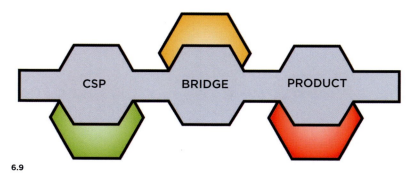

6.9

6.9
Cultural starting point or CSP is a good way to start your trend report/ presentation. The bridge is a combination of cultural references and product, leading the audience to the final part of the presentation, which is the trend product.

6.10
Use inspirational images that relate to your trend to express colour, mood and the type of consumer that the trend works best with.

library of images from various sources.

When creating a colour story, the question is often how many colours there should be in one trend forecast. It really depends on the size of the company collections and also what sector the colour palette is made for. If the colour mood is made just to give direction, it can have five to ten colours. If the colour palette is a 'working' colour palette, it would be somewhere between ten to twenty colours, on average. From the larger colour palette you can extract the smaller direction palette, a kind of colour pulse for the larger palette.

It really depends on how the colour information will be used. For example, if your audience is a menswear brand that wants to have an autumn/winter forecast with full colour, you would present four to five trends, with each trend consisting of a working colour palette of fourteen to twenty colours. The palette can then be broken down to the colour pulse of the story and then combinations. Colour combinations are important to consider because some combinations can work better than others depending on your trend. The colour usage from larger palettes is usually broken down to a main palette (colours that would be used for the main body of the article), a secondary suggestion (colours that would cover smaller parts, such as pockets, yokes or sleeves) and finally the highlight or 'pop' colour (mainly used in trims and smaller areas). Colour

is one of the most exciting parts of trends and is the most fun to work with during the translation process.

TAMARILLO

A fruity shade of Tamarillo red makes a vibrant statement in winter menswear, its concentrated tone bursting with energy.

6.10

SAMPLE COLOUR BREAKDOWN

In this example the main body and buttons of the shirt are blue, the yoke and pockets lilac and the inside of the collar stand red. For this colour usage, the blue would have been in the main palette, the lilac in the secondary and the red used only as a highlight or pop colour. Source: Author.

6.11

MATERIALS

Material stories follow hand in hand with colour stories. It is sometimes difficult to find exact matching materials for the colour, unless the company has the ability to dye textiles and garments to match. Material boards are part of the process of matching colour, but they are also important in expressing the feel and weight of the trend. Material boards are used to help in sourcing of materials and design development: for example, a footwear design team would use the information presented on the material board when buying material for future collections. It is therefore an important reference for forecasting.

6.11
Material and surface design research adds value to your trend research when you can show concrete material samples.

GRAPHIC SURFACE DESIGN

Adding graphic surface designs, such as print, is one of the easiest ways to translate a trend into a finished product. Visualization of the trend as a print is easy but should not be too obvious. Graphic trends go through the same ageing process as any trend – an example being the moustache graphic that has moved through to late majority and would not be on-trend anymore. Text as slogans or as graphic has also been used effectively by brands. Slogans can be used in advertising, online communication or even on the actual labels on the clothes to reinforce the seasonal trend. The graphics forecast section would take cues from a variety of print sources such as magazines, books, poster culture, streets and contemporary art. The surface design possibilities are endless, but it is quite easy to spot an overall trend by observing various channels (e.g., catwalks, street style, trade shows etc.).

EARLY MANIFESTATIONS

An early manifestation of the trend appears in directional or fashion forward brands and how they influence the market. For example, brands that show only a super wide trouser leg (going against the leaner silhouette) should be carefully observed in order to see if the early trend will evolve. Many bigger brands look for 'inspiration' from these brands, so they are an important signpost for many. It is a good trend-confirming point and gives more confidence to companies that might invest in the trend.

Don't forget that when you suggest that a company go with a trend, it becomes an investment. They will start developing colour, materials and final prototypes based on your prediction. It is important to have as much material as possible to support your foresight. Directional sources can be seen in many of the more established lifestyle stores the world over (e.g., Dover Street Market, London; The Broken Arm, Paris; Apartment, Berlin) or in newer retailers. The Internet is a good starting point. It is also important to visit as many retailers as possible in order to have a better understanding of the directional market in your local city.

6.12

TREND SUPPORT

A trend report can also have a selection of material from the shows to support your forecast. This can be at the end of each section, a type of 'best of shows' section. In this section you can show material samples from various shows visited, such as Linea Pelle, Pitti Filati and Première Vision, for example. The material proof needs to cross reference various types of shows, yet confirm a uniform trend seen across all the shows.

For example, if you are working on a menswear trend story that references metallics such as silver and copper tones, you would then refer to the materials shows that confirm your hunch. If more than three shows have those types of material in several vendor stands, you can assume that products will be made from those materials. The point is to prove that there is a trend emerging from the materials shows. The 'best of shows' section is also an opportunity to summarize supporting research from other areas of gathered information such as retail, and it is a way of allowing space for the more inspirational sections of your presentation.

6.12
Look for early signals of your trend in the marketplace's directional products, as seen here in Dover Street London.

6.13–6.14
Early signals can also be found in material trade shows, as seen here at Linea Pelle. If oval buckles or metallic material finishes are seen in material shows in several stands, most likely they will carry over to finished products and will possibly become a trend. Material show products are often the early manifestation of a trend.

6.13

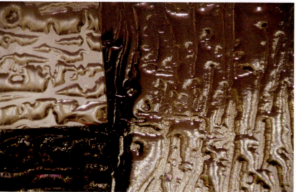

6.14

TREND-BASED PRODUCT PATHS

If working with a client such as a retailer, they will most likely want you to show sample product designs based on the trend, which they will then use as a guide for collection design. This is the most practical part of the forecast, as companies often want ideas as a type of design starting point. Again, depending on what the client wants, you can also offer full collection design and development, although this would require a whole fashion team to accomplish.

The most common approach is to offer items that help to get started with the design process. One of these items could be broken down into silhouette suggestions, with a list of detail suggestions, in order to break down what elements make the trend: 1) what silhouette to consider; 2) what details will emphasize this trend; 3) what kind of graphics are important to consider. This is the tool kit that is made for the end user.

When mixing these items with the colour and material information, you provide a menu for any brand to be able to create a strong collection with a more profound sociocultural base. This approach provides inspiration instead of copycat fashion ideas from other brands. If you present a trend to a company that is based on cultural factors, include your interpretation of these factors, thereby offering better retail variety.

TREND CONCLUSION

As in any presentation, end with a strong conclusion. The conclusion can be an overview of what was covered. This would perhaps consist of a list of key words, slogans, concepts and statements. The conclusion would also have the must-have silhouette, details, colours and materials.

A full trend forecasting package can entail a lot of work and requires material that is inspiring but also practical. If all of the elements discussed are included in a presentation, it can easily become close to 100 pages. Think of dedicating about twenty-five pages per trend – so, with four trends, you already have 100 pages. If printed copies are required, it must be calculated into the budget before starting any contractual work.

As far as timing is concerned, calculate at least a few days for each of the sections. For example, if a large amount of design work is required, you should consider whether to do it yourself, or outsource the work. One line drawing done with Illustrator can take several hours, so if a fully designed collection needs to be delivered, you need to anticipate all the extra hours of labour. A trend-forecasting package in general will take several weeks to prepare, if all researched material is already at hand.

6.15

6.15
Sometimes it is good to provide a trend product starting point on which the design team can base their models. For autumn/winter 2017 the return of the parka is predicted, and a classic parka drawing was presented for the company to base their design direction on.

TREND PRESENTATION EXERCISE

In this section we will give you general guidelines on what to include in an inspirational menswear trend forecast. You can use whatever program you like to deliver a presentation, but PowerPoint or Keynote are still the main tools. Make sure that when you export the slides to the presentation they are of a good enough quality to project, but not too large (data size-wise). The slides will be used as a presentation, as well as a printed product. The main aim of the presentation is to set the trend mood, the colour and material direction and, if needed, early product manifestations and suggestions. Each part of the following sections can be expanded and elaborated to create your own creative presentation style.

THE MOOD

The very first page will immediately set the pace for your presentation. The font, background and title will play an important role in this. A simple cover page with the name of the trend is always effective. The page can also show the name of the brand or client company to whom you are presenting, along with your name, but these optional items are a matter of taste. The important thing is that the starting page is simple and professional. Naming your trend well is also essential, since it will be referred to often during design meetings and when discussing the research. One- or two-word titles are always easy to work with and are more memorable.

The best way to set the mood for the rest of your presentation is with strong visuals. This can be a collection of images, but it is important to keep it as clear as possible, and sometimes a strong single image can do the job. There is value in imagery that is taken by you (primary research), that can be mixed with someone else's work (secondary). It is also a good idea to support your trend visuals with some text, maybe in an additional slide. This will help you to demonstrate and explain what observations the trend came from. Again, this section can be a few pages long, but no longer, to help you to explain in more detail the evidence that supports your trend vision. The text is also a good opportunity to explain what is to come in the presentation.

6.16
Always start your report with a simple title page that reflects the mood of the trend.

COLOUR AND MATERIAL

Ideally in this part of your presentation you would show an inspirational image where your colour story lives, alongside a Pantone reference palette. You can either use the pre-set Pantone names or create your own colour names. The colour names you are creating should relate to the mood and the spirit of the trend. It is important to use the correct Pantone codes – not just the names of the colours – to avoid matching problems. From this palette you can present matching materials references. It is important that a physical material reference is provided, as opposed to a digital file, in order to see how the colour 'feels' three dimensionally.

An effective way to present a colour palette is to divide it into a three-page area. The first page would be a title page that clearly separates the section from the earlier product driven section. The second page would be image/s and the colour palette that is extracted from this image – in other words, the colour palette page (obviously the image or images would relate to your trend). The third page would be a colour page, with colours matching colour referencing numbers and the colour names.

Following the colour section, create an area that references the material language. These are material direction suggestions for the trend. Also keep a record of where the material comes from; if at all possible, include the mill or tannery, as well as the prices for reference, in your presentation. This is just in case the end user (such as a brand) wants to inquire further by contacting the provider directly. Price is always a main concern for companies and brands, so this information needs to be at your fingertips. The material 'mood' does not necessarily have to totally match the colour forecast, but the closer you are with the colour the better. As mentioned earlier, if a company can dye their own materials, that is ideal.

MENSWEAR REPORT
SPRING / SUMMER 2017

6.16

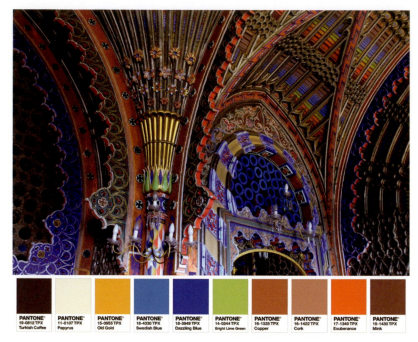

6.17

6.18

6.17
Create inspirational
colour images
yourself or have
them done
professionally
rather than using
found imagery from
the Internet. The
fact that you have
created something
yourself that is not
available to the
wider audience
adds value to your
work.

6.18
Matching the colour
and materials is
not always easy,
but definitely
adds value to your
report.

PRODUCT MANIFESTATIONS AND SUGGESTIONS

After the mood, colour and materials you can start connecting the trend with the product, creating a framework for your storytelling. Up until this point you have created an idea for your audience about how the trend could possibly manifest. In this section the trend starts to become more tangible as your present an actual product type that you have in mind for the trend.

Create a section showing early manifestations of the trend. This section should be an inspirational collage of images from retail, street style, catwalks and/or trade shows. Whichever images you decide to use, make sure you know the content fully, can discuss what is behind the image and can explain how it relates to your trend. Presenting the early manifestations of a trend allows your audience to feel confident that the observed signals are on their way to becoming a trend phenomena.

Trend companies often give silhouette and product direction suggestions demonstrating how to add the trend elements to a product. This can be done with a simple illustrated drawing that will express or illustrate the trend points discussed. In this section a detailed 'trend takeaway' page would be a good way to provide material to work with. If a more substantial collection is needed, make sure to work closely with the client to get the best possible end result.

6.19

6.20

6.19
It is good to start connecting product to your trend early because this will captivate the audience more. If you see someone wearing colours or an accessory, as seen here, that connects to your trend, show it. Street-style sometimes can provide good trend confirmation.

6.20
Include a materials story that relates to your trend. Collect as many samples as possible from seasonal shows so that you have them when you need them.

PRESENTATION CONCLUSION

Use the last section as a must-have takeaway page for the trend that summarizes all the information that you have shown. These pages are especially good for reviewing the trend information with your audience. The conclusion section can be a type of chart, or a list of key points to consider. The presentation can be very long and should be packed with information (on average, a trend section takes thirty minutes to present); therefore, it makes sense to have all the key information in one page at the end. The very last page of your presentation should include contact information and legalities such as copyright information.

WORKSHOP EXERCISE: HOW TO RUN A CORPORATE TREND WORKSHOP

A trend workshop provides an opportunity to introduce trends in a more hands-on way. A workshop can be very beneficial in helping clients to better understand how trends can be applied. It also makes for a fun classroom activity. Ideally a trend workshop would take one day, with a morning session dedicated to the informational and inspirational trend presentation and the afternoon dedicated to workshops. During these workshops participants can explore how to apply the trend in their given department.

SPACE

WANDERER

HABITAT

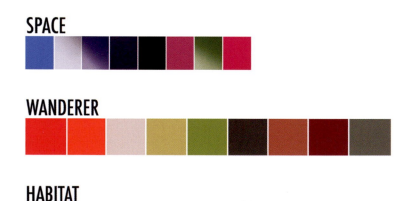

GO GLO

THE WORKSHOP

Start your workshop with four or five trends – each trend should take about thirty minutes to present. For example, if you have four presentations, you should allocate two hours to present just the trends. Show the early signals of the trend with plenty of inspirational images. Include also video material that supports your trend. Make sure to include colour information in each trend section, explaining each colour in depth and how it relates to the trend.

The trend forecast in the morning presentation should not only be inspirational, but also needs to be packed with concrete workable information, such as silhouette, material, product suggestions and so on. Brands and companies often ask 'what is next?' and ' what is new?'. It is your job and responsibility to deliver this information throughout the workshop. Ensure that the participants take careful notes on each presentation as well as jotting down concepts, keywords and initial ideas that come to their minds about how to apply the trends. As a presenter and facilitator, you can help by writing out some key ideas throughout your presentation. Use only high quality visuals and materials of which you have a full understanding.

For the afternoon workshop divide the audience into groups. If there are fewer than eight people, select two trends to work on. Otherwise, if you have four trends, make four groups (or four pairs). Before making the groups, find out what the job profiles are. If there are merchandisers, buyers and designers taking part, make groups that are a mix of different areas of expertise. After assigning the trends to groups, work with each group individually. Each group will need to present the outcome of the trend at the end of the afternoon. What the groups first need to look at is the trend and how can it be applied to the brand. It is interesting to give the groups liberty to work on areas that they are not normally involved with. A buyer can have a great trend driven idea for visual merchandising and vice versa. The point of the workshop is to be exposed to trends and try to figure out how to apply the information to a given department or sector. Look at some trends and have a quick brainstorm with a group to see how the information can be applied to various areas of your future position. To help with a group's thought process, provide some guidelines to help them get started. The following questions should be asked: What area of your business do you think the trend is most suitable for? What is the customer profile of the person who would use this trend?

6.21
The last page is the takeaway, or a summary of the all the trends in the report. Here is a summary of the four colour palettes that allow a client to have a good overview and select a few trends to work on.

6.22

GENERAL PRESENTATION TECHNIQUES

One of the most important aspects of trend forecasting is being able to clearly communicate a trend to an audience. Some people perform well in front of an audience, others not so well, and some are even afraid. Stage fright is something that will go away the more you gain experience, and sometimes a little nervousness can be good. The main thing to remember is not to be insecure because your audience will sense this immediately. If you know your material inside out, then you should be fully confident. You are presenting something you specialize in.

Do not read the whole presentation. It is perfectly fine to keep some notes to help you to remember the main points, but reading the full presentation is dull. It is also important to engage with the audience: ask occasional questions, encourage them to provide opinions. However, do not have a constant conversation. Take the lead and be in charge of the presentation.

A trend workshop is an effective way to accomplish a fuller understanding of trend and trend forecasting. The workshop is not only limited to corporate presentations, but also can be used in executive training and in a classroom environment. A workshop can also be done in a shorter time and with fewer trends, but the framework works the best with the given schedule.

Key presentation techniques are:
• Practice the content and do not leave it to the last minute.
• Time it well and engage the audience.
• Know your material inside out.
• Do not read your presentation.
• Provide facts and figures.
• Be confident.
• Speak clearly.
• Avoid jargon.
• Have a strong start and end to your presentation.

6.22
Workshop benefits include providing opportunities for creative exploration and gives the participants a great way to not only think with their heads but also use their hands as well, as seen here at a Trendstop workshop.

6.23

SANDY MACLENNAN
CEO East Central Studios

MacLennan studied textile design in the 1970s and then joined a leading London design consultancy, managing a team of designers to develop the Japanese market. In 1982, he set up East Central Studios, a design studio specializing in colour forecasting, textiles, fashion design and the associated promotion, marketing and branding. MacLennan is known for his scope of expertise in this colour field. In 1995, his studio co-created the design and marketing magazine *Viewpoint* and acted as a creative director until Issue 10. He is also a contributing trend editor for *Textile View* magazine.

Why colour? When I first started my career at a London design studio, Deryck Healey International, in the 1970s I became fascinated by the British Colour Authority Archive, which Deryck had acquired after the organization disbanded.

It was an enormous and complex physical reference of every product category you can imagine – from men's hats and ribbon trims, to women's hosiery, silks and woollens. It was fascinating to see the steady progress and adoption of one colour over another through the seasons, and that inspired me to take part in that studio's work to inaugurate the BTCG (British Textile Colour Group) again. It was mainly about womenswear, and I began to work on the menswear area. From there, I have maintained a role in that group now for over thirty years now.

The BTCG is a not-for-profit group that has grown over the years to approximately thirty members, all independent consultants, plus some commercial organizations who pay a premium to be part of it.

We meet two years ahead of the season and you present your first thoughts in front of your peer group. It's a tentative and explorative moment for everyone, and it often produces a surprising outcome that is then carried forward to an international meeting where the process is repeated . . . And the outcome of all this can sometimes be easily seen at venues like Première Vision and the collections you see there.

It's a kind of self-fulfilling prophecy . . . After that each individual (including me) leverages something from this process in their own commercial work. In my case it would be working with John Smedley, for example, to determine each season's colour selection for their fine luxury knitwear ranges.

I also work on the View Pantone Colour Planner, which is published eighteen months ahead of the season.

What is the meaning/significance of colour in the marketplace today? I think for everyone, it is the starting pistol for the season's race. Real newness is often edited to a minimum while reflecting on what sold last season; often it's about a 'refreshment' or a progression. Consumers love what they love and often return to their favourites. Some brands leverage this well, using 'their' colours and variations

6.23
Sandy MacLennan is a world-leading textile and colour specialist.

6.24

in a minimal strategic way; others rely on it as a loss leader to draw their customer in.

So for me I think successful brands/ businesses have to know their customer's preferences and favourites and respond with just enough newness to excite them and challenge them while delivering the familiar codes they feel good about. It's like, you always know what Paul Smith will re-present each season – same for Burberry. Conversely, Raf Simons is someone who uses colour surgically and with aplomb, always breaking the rules a little to keep you on your toes.

In short, I really believe that a business involved in making products cannot ignore the power and significance of colour as a springboard, as the first point of contact, for new ideas and products. The consumer public can sense and see good innovations, and colour helps to call their attention to that newness.

What is the relationship of menswear and colour? In the past, men's colour was a very slow and steady progression, and each season there was a known code, an understood limit on what was expected for menswear. It was almost as though each season was a version of something that was always there – how navy was moving, what tone and timbre there were to greys etc.

Today I can see that menswear has a more volatile and confident approach to colour, but without the 'fashiony' modes of womenswear. Good collections are rational but inspired, shot through with accents or confident solids that can be enjoyed by everyone. It's a process of playing with colours that rocks between dramatic and restrained – never going too far. Everyone knows catwalk and stylists push the boundaries, but there is always a way to balance and interpret the season in a way that appeals to the avant-garde as well as the everyman.

How do you start your colour work? I first believe you have to just feel it. You have to allow yourself to be drawn to something that intrigues you or appeals. This can be a visual game or a word game. I often make up colour narratives out of just words. From here I try to visualize something that embodies that storyline, often relying on found images, but sometimes by painting, inking and pigmenting pure colour onto materials. This way I feel you invent colour rather than just referencing it. Tom Ford said new ideas come out of a process where he first throws away everything he is bored with and looks at what's left. What's left is what interests him going forward. We all have to find our own process for generating newness.

6.24
Material references bring tactile dimension to the colour mood of your presentation.

6.25
Text supporting the imagery and colour palette can provide a good opening for your colour story.

6.26
Colour forecasts give companies professional suggestions on what combinations work the best.

6.27
A mixture of illustration, collage and textile samples make a captivating spread, as seen here in *Textile View*.

6.28
Images accompanying the textile story will help to visualize the mood and feel of the story.

6.25

6.26

In practical terms how do you work with companies?

Depending on your relationship, it can be quite quick and systematic. For example, with the designers at John Smedley, I show them my workings to date, my stories in raw, first form, the feedback from the BTCG, and I describe how people (my peer group) are thinking about colours. How important a yellow was, what is happening to blue, or the plethora of greens around (often a sign of indecision!) And from here we determine a series of potential colour 'families'. There will be five reds, four blues, six turquoise that go from greens to blues and greys etc. These first 'matchings' will then be taken to the lab and dyed onto the correct materials/yarns, and often each dye match will have three versions to choose from.

We then have another meeting to review them, assessing each individually and then together as a whole. Then there is a brutal edit to perhaps twenty-four in total, including all the classics. And here we even separate women's and men's – some doubling up in each. It is a straightforward process that results in a new palette that gets put into sample garments and merchandised at the salons (Pitti Uomo etc.). Colour is the driver for their whole production.

With other clients it may be as simple as producing a slick colour card with text and a visual to accompany their communication of an idea (e.g., for fibre companies) who are not 'selling' colour but using it as an introductory voice for their product to differentiate itself. It is about confidence and service. Give people something useful and you can build the concept of customer loyalty into the commercial mix.

Or – you make a larger, more dramatic and full visual presentation of colour themes and ideas that are designed to inspire a creative internal team to work on their seasons ranges differently. Not to be didactic, but just to be inspiring. This is often seen as a springboard or a relay race where you pass the baton onwards to the next player in the chain. The outcomes here are harder to quantify, but with time the targets become more refined and the success rate is more evident.

6.27

6.28

6.29

What is your point of view on digital colour versus material colour? Digital colour is fine for a quick communication and ease of sharing a message. Sometimes it's only about a feel and a look, but you can secure it if you code match to a system like Pantone. But for actual product development innovation you need to work with material 'matchings'. There is nothing to beat it. The nuance and shape shifting that goes on when you apply colour to a substrate is a volatile process. Everything needs to be reviewed as it goes along, and a good edit will often create the final perfect tension needed to let products come alive.

What are the basics to consider when researching colour trends? A good eye. Good context and a firm background on what everyone else in your world is doing with colour. From this natural reference point you can let your own ideas come forward with a confidence that means you understand the context of ideas, tonalities and contrasts. You have to acknowledge the current narratives, but move appropriately forward to meet the challenge of your target (client, product, communication).

Giving voice to these stories is key. Words, image making, selection and editing are all part of the motivational process that gets your ideas adopted the way you imagined. Hone your instincts. Feel it.

Many students are interested in specializing in 'colour' as a career. What path do you recommend? It depends where in the supply chain they want to work. If they are in love with a brand, designer or retailer, they have to engage with them. Learn all they can about them and speak to them however they like. It's hard but if they are dedicated to it (and 5 per cent will be) they will manage. From here they will be in a known process of intel planning with their preferred suppliers, about eighteen to fifteen months ahead. If they want to become independent colour consultants, they need also to start on the bottom rung. Maybe in media – or with a design group would be a start. Curiosity is the weapon of choice. If they don't have it, they should go into another sphere.

6.29
When compiling a magazine editorial, reference the textile samples clearly and give credit accordingly, as seen here in *Textile View* magazine.

What are the latest developments in colour technologies? To be honest, I leave the tech side of things to another conversation. I am purely interested in colour for colour itself. Of course I am aware of current restrictions coming in where some colours just won't be allowed any more (Fluo etc.) because of their harmful metal contents. But other fields of interest blend with a more sustainable obsession. Like how to dye without using water – or how to mimic colours with refraction like a butterfly wing. There are a lot of things on the drawing board and even being commercialized. These are amazing current developments becoming a reality and it is easy to see how they could 'inspire' colouration ideas and trends, but they don't drive the actuality of my choices. They don't always mean a lot to Joe Blow either. He just wants something cool and sharp. The story is interesting but maybe not enough to pay extra for it!

How do you see menswear developing in the future? It's always a step-by-step process. Then there are some minor explosions of innovation that catch your attention, but when it arrives at retail it is usually something we recognize and understand. Menswear more fits with 'types' rather than imposing a fashion 'trend' onto the masses.

Men are much more willing to play the game now. There is scope for a very fluid interpretation of traditional codes. Summer is always a time for something frivolous and winter brings out investment buying. There is a lot of instant cheap visual 'value' retailing going on in parallel to a more quality driven purchase. It is a game of two halves – of two tribes. It always will be a dichotomy, but now more than ever there is a serious consideration, at fabric mill level, to bring innovation to the fore. It is more evident in menswear because of its simplicity. In womenswear there is so much to think about it drowns itself in ideas, but with the modern man of the future, I think there is a much more steady and rational approach to appreciating the new and relevant ideas circulating in fashion today.

6.30
When showing colour stories next to one another, you can clearly see the difference in the mood and their possible end use.

6.30

CHAPTER SUMMARY

In this chapter we have demonstrated how to turn trend data into a trend product in the form of the trend report, which is the summary of your trend research, and trend workshop, which provides a more hands-on approach on how to use trend information. Individuals and companies use this information differently, yet the approaches demonstrated can be applied to various situations and scenarios. For example, the trend report is useful for textile and leather manufacturers to produce on-trend material collections and for designers to inspire collections that men will want to wear in the future. The trend report is a powerful tool to help buyers and merchandisers to make educated strategic decisions. In short, a trend report in its various versions will help menswear businesses to stay ahead of the competition.

A workshop is ideal to practice how to take trends and translate them to workable items. A workshop can be beneficial to a large design team that needs a directional guideline for the collection design. The workshop can also help broaden the views of an audience that includes non-creative professionals. It is up to the workshop organizer to set the parameters and make the workshop into an inspirational opportunity to explore new ways of thinking.

This chapter also covered some basic presentation techniques. When working with something as vast and sometimes intangible as trends, it is absolutely vital that your presentation is clear, inspirational and confident. Making presentations in public can be a source of stress for many, but, as with any skill, practice makes perfect.

HOMEWORK ASSIGNMENTS

1. Create a materials board with a colour reference board.
2. Research a company and choose two or three trends you think would help them the most.
3. Create a still life with fruit or objects and create a colour story out of it.

DISCUSSION ACTIVITIES AND PROJECTS

1. Select five inspirational colour images. Then see if you can extract colour stories suitable for menswear.
2. Research a trend and have a small workshop in class to discuss various scenarios to ally the information to.
3. Create either a full trend forecast or sectional (mood, colour etc.) presentation.
4. Record your presentation and analyse.

KEY WORDS

bridge
cultural starting point (CSP)
Pantone
presentation
trend deliverables
workshop

7.1

7.1
Creative agencies offer good opportunities for someone with a trend background. Trade shows often have a trend agency presence, as shown here with Fashion Snoops. This makes trade shows a good place to review what different trend services offer.

7

Trends and the Industry

LEARNING OBJECTIVES

- Explore the various job roles within the trend industry.
- Differentiate between trend services.
- Identify existing professional roles.
- Create a cover letter and a CV.
- Navigate the contemporary job market.
- Illustrate your skills in a portfolio.

INTRODUCTION

Trends appear in various sectors of the menswear industry, from retail to menswear publications. Trend information is channelled to retailers either from full service trend agencies and freelancers or from in-house trend analysts. These analysts gather information from the Internet, magazines and retail. Each of these channels offers various professional opportunities for a fashion and design graduate with trend experience. When scanning international job postings that include design, buying or merchandising jobs, knowledge of trends is often required. 'Market data' and 'consumer insight' are also terms used in describing trend behaviour.

One can become a full-time trend forecaster or analyst, but the job market is not limited to trend agencies alone. Even when brands do not specifically advertise trend knowledge requirements, the basic understanding of trend reasoning and methodology proves to be useful.

Trend agencies are the most obvious starting point for researching opportunities in the trend job market: several industry insights have been included throughout the book in order to provide a better understanding of the menswear trend market. Beyond trend agency opportunities, there are various other places that use and can benefit from trend knowledge. Industry trade shows have specific trend areas that are often outsourced from trend companies. However, sometimes trade shows may have their own internal teams that create trend areas. These areas often include trend presentations open to exhibition participants. In addition to trade shows, there are also trade magazines (for example, textile and colour magazines) that have a need for staff with a trend background. Becoming a freelancer is also a possibility, but as in any freelance path, it can be difficult to obtain the initial experience required to work in this role. As such, it is advisable to gain some experience before setting out to become a free agent.

THE JOB HUNT

A question often asked is, 'How do I find employment in this field?' You first need to narrow down your skills and interests (i.e., what type of work have you been trained in? what type of work best suits you? and, most importantly, what can you offer to a prospective employer?). Job postings are always a good starting point; you will find these online. Look into portals such as drapersjobs.com and stylecareers.com to check the current demand for trend jobs. In addition, online business networking is abundant in today's world, with sites such as linkedin.com helping to connect job seekers with possible employers.

Another route to find positions is to search through company websites. Brands, trend agencies and retailers alike post positions on their own websites. Networking in person is also important. Take advantage of every opportunity to go and meet people; have your business cards ready! Registering with job agencies is also a good idea, but be wary of any website or agency that wants to charge you a fee as usually it is the hiring company that pays a reputable agency after a position has been filled.

TREND PROFESSIONAL ROLES

There are a number of professional roles in the fashion trend industry, as outlined below. In addition to these, you may find many opportunities in different design fields because global job postings often require trend knowledge in the design and marketing areas of the fashion industry.

TREND ANALYST/ FORECASTER

The most common job role in the fashion trend industry is the trend analyst/forecaster. The main activity for a person in this role is to study the marketplace, see what type of product is emerging from it and figure out how to translate the information to the company (see Chapter 3's 'Industry Insight' with Ember Todd). The analyst monitors global catwalk activity, street styling, trade show reporting and social media activity. Part of the analysis entails looking at what is happening on the retail front in order to analyse what is offered in stores and online (i.e., brick and mortar as well as e-tailing).

Day to day work often includes information organizational tasks, such as catwalk image tagging using various key words for easier access. The forecasting aspect of the job involves taking all of the information researched in order to create a suggestion (i.e., a forecast based on this data).

COLOUR AND MATERIAL SPECIALIST

Most larger footwear and apparel companies employ a person who is strictly responsible for colour and material direction. The two specialties can also be separate jobs within a company. The colour specialist would deal with colour selection and its application to the product, whether it is footwear, accessories or apparel. The colour specialist would get cues from many sources as varied as food trends and the colour producers and reference systems, such as Pantone. Colour specialism is a vital part of any fashion company, since it is one of the main factors deciding consumer purchases.

FREELANCER

Although full-time trend positions are available, the more flexible opportunities are in freelancing. To be a freelance trend analyst, it is essential to have some prior experience. This can be gained through internship or work placement opportunities. Information gathering tasks, such as exhibition or street style reporting, also present an opportunity to gain experience and are a good entry point to trend agencies and magazines. This experience can be utilized to initiate a solid portfolio.

As a freelancer, it is important to take into consideration that trend work and consulting are time consuming. Depending on the size or the requirements of the consultancy, you will most likely be unable to manage it all on your own. Delegation of work is frequently required, which is why it is important to develop a good working relationship with possible associates – you will often need their assistance on projects. However, if hired for trend projects inside menswear companies, you will most likely be producing one portion of the trend package (as part of a larger team). One of the most demanded end products in design is colour and material knowledge and the ability to report on it. On the business of fashion side, trend work is focused on consumer trends and what the menswear market may require.

7.2
Trend agencies such as Fashion Snoops are the ideal work environments for a trend professional. Here, Michael Fisher, Creative Director of Menswear at Fashion Snoops, reviews seasonal colour information.

ADDITIONAL ROLES

Additional roles that benefit from trend studies are futurist/futurologist, consumer strategist and creative/art director. A futurist or futurologist usually focuses on the mega trends and looks at the world several decades or centuries ahead. These types of job positions do not appear often, but organizations such as the Copenhagen Institute of Future Studies are a good starting point.

TREND AGENCY JOB OPPORTUNITIES

Trend agencies are companies that provide trend intelligence to global audiences. They are the largest employer of trend professionals, with a growing need for menswear trend specialists.

Trend agencies have their signature styles and often specialize in something in order to have a competitive edge. All trend agencies share common categories, such as catwalk, street style, colour and general trend direction. Agencies such as WGSN, Trendstop and Fashion Snoops offer both creative trend directions as well as tailored consulting services. Their main channel of communication is through the Internet, using various digital platforms and password enabled services. Agencies that are less technology driven, such as Paris-based Trend Union, led by the trend visionary Lidewij Edelkoort, focus on material. Their services are based on seasonal global trend presentations that are accompanied by books with colour cards and actual material samples. There are also many agencies around the globe that specialize in their own geographical markets, or more specific areas of interest, such as footwear or sportswear. In addition, newly established agencies such as Trend Atelier and K-Hole present a fresh view and delivery on trends.

All agencies require various skilled professionals in their workforce and one of the best ways to secure a job in an agency is via the internship route. Explore job opportunities at trend agencies through the careers sections of their websites; many of them may have open positions.

7.2

7.3

areas are often outsourced from trend agencies, but they also do employ freelancers. Find the closest material trade show. Many companies have international editions to reach clients who cannot or do not want to travel. Look at the show's website to gain a better understanding of who is in charge of the show's trend content. Although trade shows are primarily intended for business activities, they also provide a good networking opportunity for graduates. If visiting a trade show is not a possibility, contact the show producers online (see Chapter 5 for trade show contacts).

TRADE SHOW JOB OPPORTUNITIES

Trade shows, especially material shows, offer trend information to the show attendees, advising what material directions to invest in. Trade shows such as Linea Pelle present a trend area that is the first stop for visitors to observe colour predictions and material tables. Shows such as The Première Vision have trend presentations that support the show's direction, as well as many vendors with material in stands to assist buyers.

In addition, shows such as ISPO (Sports), Micam (Shoes) and Mipel (Bags) all have specific trend presentations that may entice clients to buy into trends. The trade show world is a good place to explore opportunities in trend forecasting because most shows have a trend area. These

PUBLICATION JOB OPPORTUNITIES

Publications such as magazines employ freelance contributors and also sometimes hire trend specialists. This is often the case with trade magazines, such as all the *View* publications or *Mix* magazine, published by Global Colour Research. Garment trade magazines, such as *Sportswear International*, *Collezioni* and *Zoom on Fashion Trends* have trend-driven content, and menswear magazines such as *GQ* and *Details* have global distribution. In addition to these more mainstream publications, there are various lesser-known menswear publications, such as *Man About Town* magazine and *MITT*. All these companies need professionals that understand trends, making them an attractive prospect for someone interested in trend and printed communication.

7.3
Trade shows often have trend areas, as seen here in one of several halls of Linea Pelle, the world's leading leather show.

One of the most influential men's publications is the London-based *Monocle* magazine. They recently launched an annual report called the Forecast that suggests which are the most important places, people and brands. It is a type of global guide book showing how to stay ahead of the menswear game.

In addition to magazines, there are an array of trend books that are for sale either in bookstores or at various trade shows. Books such as *Next Look*, *Style Right* and printed publications from Scout and Trend Union can vary in price from several hundred to thousands of pounds. Trade shows are one of the best places to research trend books, usually at the show bookstores. However, the one-stop shop for trend books and trend-related fashion magazines is modeinfo.com, where you can see details of all the above-mentioned publications.

Again, the best way to approach the magazines is to contact them directly. Go to the magazine's website to see if there is human resources or career information. Call them for more detailed information. When calling magazines, try to get the name of a person to address your portfolio and CV to.

7.4

RETAIL JOB OPPORTUNITIES

Retail is a large sector, but any employee in a retail role that involves fashion should be well versed in trend knowledge. Working as a trend specialist inside a retail company would most likely mean that you would conduct research to create trend reports for the retailer. This could be a combination of 'comparative shopping' (when you buy competing brand products), monitoring data from trend agencies, and personal retail and consumer research. Reporting to various departments' heads will help them to make more competitive decisions regarding their strategy.

7.4
Magazines, such as *View*, usually hire freelancers to create trends editorials, making it an ideal place to express individual style.

7.5

7.5
Menswear
retail, in various
forms, presents
trend-driven
opportunities from
merchandising
to buying, as
seen here with
Brooks Brothers
recently tapping
into contemporary
trends.

TREND AGENCY START-UP

Before starting your own business, first obtain experience in all trend sectors, such as research, trend deliverables and presentations. You have to also be able to effectively network and offer something unique in this heavily competitive market. Trend agencies are a non-regulated business, so having a professional identity will set you apart from the amateur practitioners.

The first step in starting any type of business is to formulate a business plan. Online you will find an abundance of samples and templates, but it is always good to get face-to-face advice on your business plan as well. Banks and independent advisors can also assist you with business planning. The plan will mainly help you to determine how much you need to earn – first of all, to cover your costs, but ultimately to gain profit. You will need to be able to ascertain how much your daily running costs will be – from the operating space (whether brick and mortar or virtual space) to printing and production costs. A good way to start gathering business plan information is to create a simple list. Opposite are some guidelines that will help you with the plan and help you to decide if having your own business is viable.

As previously mentioned, many companies have an internal trend analyst or even an entire department dedicated to searching for the latest signals and consumer data. Department stores use trend intelligence information all the time, from visual merchandising to buying. The most effective way to break into the retail business is to monitor online job postings for possible opportunities, either through checking the retailer's website career section or by visiting online job portals such as drapersjobs.com or stylecareers.com.

START-UP CHEAT SHEET

- Time: What are the projected hours required for each project? What is your projected salary?
- Legalities: You will need to have a name for trading purposes and all related permissions.
- Branding: You will need to have a catchy name (that is not currently traded under) and take care of all related legalities from trademarking to business registrations.
- Graphics: The branding and other graphic content needs to be designed.
- Online: Having an online presence is essential today. Website and social media need to be built, maintained and loaded with enticing content.
- Photography: You will need a photographer to provide high quality content for your work. This can vary from street styling to material swatches.
- Copywriting: There is nothing worse than a document with badly written text.
- Printing: Printing is always needed, even if just for internal office use.
- Business cards: Stationery and other office communication materials will be necessary.
- Hardware: This covers technology such as desktops, laptops, printers and scanners.
- Insurance: What type of insurance, if any, is needed?
- Travel: How much travel is required for the agency? Travel often becomes the main expense for small fashion businesses.
- Staff: Will there be staff? If so, what are the labour requirements for hiring?
- Accountant: Accounting can get complicated when business invoicing is involved (not to mention salaries).
- Shipping costs: Will there be shipping costs involved?
- Business banking: What are the charges for banking?
- Material costs: What are the material costs?
- Advertising costs: Are you going to strictly use social media outlets or also advertise (which can be costly)? The basic question is: how will you acquire clients?
- Website costs: How much does website building cost?

7.6

7.7

HOW TO PREPARE FOR THE JOB MARKET

There are more fashion graduates than there are design jobs, making the fashion job market very competitive. Having trend behaviour experience will make you more marketable, whether you study design or fashion marketing. In today's job market it is no longer enough to be a visionary. You will also need to have some practical skills in order to make it in the fashion business. To launch a career and find a job, you will need to be able to write a cover letter, organize a good CV and present a strong portfolio.

CURRICULUM VITAE (CV)

The CV is a document that chronicles your professional career and achievements, and it should be clear and to the point, ideally no longer than two pages. If you are a recent graduate, add your professionally related projects to make your CV more credible.

There are many different ways a CV can be composed. Examples are available online with specific regional variances. The generic standard should show your name and contact details at the top. The first paragraph may be a short summary or profile that is six to eight sentences long and describes you as a professional person. Following the introduction might be a list of your professional accomplishments. It is also good to list exhibitions and any other participation or membership in professionally significant associations.

In North America and the UK, it is not the norm to include a photograph, while some continental European countries still require it. For most job applications, it is better to leave the photograph out (unless specifically requested). Try to avoid gimmicky and overly designed CVs. Opinions are often formed within seconds, and first impressions count; therefore, the more clear and universally understood your style is, the better your chance to impress.

COVER LETTER

A cover letter is designed to present a positive and enthusiastic first impression. Occasionally, companies will not request a cover letter, but it is good to have one for the majority of cases. The cover letter should be somewhere between 200 to 300 words. Do not include detailed work information, as this should already appear in your CV. The letter should simply state why you are applying for the job and why they should consider you. Then it should briefly describe some work history. It is also a good idea to have your contact details in the letter, just in case it gets separated from your CV. Search for various local sample cover letters online that you may use as a guideline because the style and format may vary by country.

7.6
If you start your own consultancy, make sure to be able to deliver professional illustrations alongside the creative vision. In this example the material swatches are accompanied with a clear illustration to demonstrate how to use them in menswear.

7.7
Something to consider when starting an independent service agency is the high cost of travel. For example, visiting trade shows to gather trend information, as seen here in the form of swatches from Linea Pelle, makes travel a necessary expense.

7.8

PORTFOLIO

A portfolio is a valuable tool to demonstrate your creativity to a potential employer or client. It is important to put your best work first; opinions are formed after the first few moments of opening the portfolio, so first impressions count. A portfolio should be made in both digital and printed formats. The trend portfolio should present work you have produced previously either as course work or professionally. Show the variety of skills you have, from art directing to the selection of images. The trend examples should be different in style, in order to demonstrate your ability to do different types of work. For example, there can be a spread on sportswear, or another trend on classic with a focus on fabrics. Printed portfolios will also serve as an effective tool to help you with storytelling. When presenting creative work to companies, remember that they likely are looking for a future staff member that has a clear overall understanding of menswear business activity. A portfolio should demonstrate your ability to think and perform various tasks that might be needed in a creative office.

INTERVIEW

Some basic rules apply to job interviews. The first thing to do is to research the company thoroughly. Develop a full and comprehensive idea of what it does and represents. Try to find out what the atmosphere of the company is – whether it is casual or formal – and dress accordingly. Be prepared, be enthusiastic (but not desperate) and try to come across as natural as possible. If your interviewer is comfortable with you, the rest of the process will most likely be smooth as well. Clearly explain what your experience and strengths are and how you think the company could benefit from your expertise. Also be prepared to answer the dreaded 'weaknesses' question. One way to answer this question is by looking at something that is not in your CV that you are willing/able to learn in the new job.

7.8
Portfolios can vary in size; however, they need to be simple and clean so as not to take away from the content.

7.9–7.10
The portfolio contents should show the ability to put together ideas with or without computers. In this example the tactile trend ideas are shown in a collage with material and colour sketches followed by very clear line drawings.

7.9–7.10

7.11

GERALDINE WHARRY
Future Trends and Design Consultant, Founder of Trend Atelier

Geraldine Wharry works with companies in the style industries to anticipate future design trends and create commercially successful and innovative product. Her experience, both as a hands-on fashion designer and trend forecaster, means that her visions are seamlessly commercialized into design across industry sectors as varied as fashion, interiors, electronics and retail. Through tailored insights, Geraldine Wharry helps clients update existing product and realize the potential of new design.

After studying at Duperré in Paris, she designed bestselling collections in New York and Los Angeles for leading fashion brands such as 7 For All Mankind, Triple 5 Soul and Ripcurl through a mix of innovation and pragmatism. Subsequently in London she gravitated to trend forecasting within the leading companies in this field – Wgsn, Stylus – and still conducts research for them.

Now a successful, London-based consultant, garnering industry awards and a substantial online following with her inspiration platform Trend Atelier, Geraldine works with clients across three continents, helping them shape their future through big-picture design thinking.

What was your first connection to trends and trend forecasting? I first became familiar with trends and trend forecasting services when I started my career as a fashion designer. At the start of each season, myself and the design team had to spend time (usually around one to two weeks) doing design research in order to define next season's concept, theme, colour palette and fabric direction. The time was often limited – the fashion world is so fast paced – so we would book appointments with trend agencies to buy their seasonal forecasts. They helped us layer in more design intelligence into our design research as well as gave us extra affirmation that we were going in the right direction, the kind of confidence you had to also show to managers and executives when backing up your design choices during presentations. We would look at services such as WGSN or Peclers to define what the key silhouettes were for the next season or find thought-provoking images for our mood boards. Not all our research came from trend forecasts; designers already have a naturally savvy antenna when it comes to their trend intuition. But working with trend agencies definitely made our lives easier. We didn't have weeks on hand to research so being able to rely on teams that do that full time was great. Then when I evolved into trend forecasting, it was an exciting step as I used to admire the amount of research trend forecasters could do and now I was one of them. For designers the concept part is sometimes the most fulfilling, as that's when you can let your mind wonder, question, discover new sources of inspiration, which is the step before having to deal with tech packs, button sizes and factories, although the process that goes into making product is very enthralling as well.

7.11
Geraldine Wharry translates her findings into designs through prints, sketches and garment customizations.

7.12

What is your methodology (research and development to workable trend)?

I call my methodology 'hunting and gathering'. It's a combination of visual research, factual intelligence and instinct. My trend reporting and advisory is done through research for which I stay connected with everything that is influencing design, mindsets and lifestyle: from exhibitions, to trade shows, popular culture to socioeconomics, technology to science, health and consumer behaviours – including generational influences. I also follow or consult with industry experts and global and/ or regional opinion leaders.

I then gather the research and group it into three to four directions, sometimes two, it depends (I don't shoehorn things). Usually those themes already were emerging as I was hunting for research. This is quite an important step as it requires your editing judgment. It can be a tricky side of the process: more and more trends blend into each other and it's harder to differentiate them.

The final process, which differs depending on the trend service, but I will discuss my own here, is to translate my findings into designs through prints, sketches and garment customizations in my collection 'SERIES'. The designer in me has never gone away, so my service provides the customized product application to match the trend vision and forecast so it's both a conceptual and hands-on circle of innovation.

What are the biggest mega trends for the coming years?

There are a couple of big ideas flourishing at the moment; it's an interesting eco-system.

One of the trends is for autumn/winter 2016/17 and I call it 'Modesty Solutions'. It reflects a need to convey a sense of seeking calm and balance through multidisciplinary craft as well as a more tolerant and thoughtful society. Designers echo this need through intentionally imperfect creations that combine man-made and natural materials. There is a movement for downsizing and looking into objects that are simpler to bank on fundamental functionalities and the use of essential or unconventional materials. There is also a nostalgic quality to 'Modesty Solutions', a sentimental narrative that delves back into the great depression and the 1940s. This leads to a resurgence of workwear, utility and military garments made to last as a reaction against throwaway culture. So there is a reaction against over-consumption of trends and a move towards simplifying the message – going back to basics. There is a serene quality to this trend, which also focuses on an altruistic approach to life, seeking to change pre-conceived ideas of what's imperfect and reconsider notions of equality. So we examine equality across genders, across race, women's rights, fathers' rights. It's about shifting the focus and stepping into someone else's shoes and having empathy. This trend explores an egalitarian and emotionally mature society. There is also an element of anti-establishment statements, the third wave of feminism and self body image.

7.12
'The other big change has been in the homogenization of womenswear and the mix and matching of trends within one look or collection.' Geraldine Wharry.

Another trend I called 'Wonder Wander'. It paves the way for new belief systems where designers, artists, coders and engineers collaborate to explore the meaning of cultural heritage, human connection and digital interactivity. This is an individual centric trend looking at the new 'self help' and how we can experience our spirituality, happiness, anxieties, self-image through holistic digital avenues and ingenious ways of connecting with our deeper selves. A need to escape our everyday and seek significance prevails, reflecting the growing shift of consumers towards lifestyle and drug-free mind altering experiences.

This trend also taps into video game aesthetics, as we explore new virtual environments and cities, considering never-before-seen ways of connecting with leisure-as the virtual becomes a palpable reality and shapes a not-so-distant experience of the everyday.

Finally, there is a very playful aesthetic, which is strong and updates the postmodern influence we've been seeing for several years. It experiments with intentionally messy and humorous concepts and combines them with modular design structures. This trend is inspired by toy design and explores theatricality. It looks at the spontaneous quality of performance and music, drawing these playful concepts even into the realm of more serious concerns around survival, sustainability and death. It also links the idea of serendipity with technology concepts and new ways of surfing the Internet or using our digital devices. So here we look at hacked objects, clumsy shapes made clever, the freedom of customizable design and the spontaneity of childhood, seeking to celebrate unpredictability into currently formatted views on dressing, beauty and everyday objects. This direction explores the idea of 'beautiful ugly' and is interesting for beauty concepts as well.

What is the importance of menswear at the moment? The growth of the men's fashion market has outpaced that of womenswear for at least five years, and gender roles are changing extremely fast. In the UK, also, men spend more on shoes than women and the new generation of men is more sophisticated, design and product savvy. Menswear has always followed some trends, but they were slower to change and more conservative, having little to do with runway or magazine trends. But now the menswear catwalk shows have become a major event – also for trend forecasters like myself researching emerging talent and innovative design. There is a lot of creativity coming out of menswear right now with designers such as Craig Green, Christopher Raeburn, Hood By Air and Raf Simons. The Internet has also played a major role for several reasons. One, style inspiration no longer comes from a few magazines; it is instant and global. Two, men love shopping online; e-commerce is a good formula for them. Because of a growing market demand, more and more labels are offering menswear product with their own dedicated menswear stores. In general men are very open about investing in themselves and their appearance, they are very good at finding niche product, which ranges from technology to clothing and grooming. In a recent article I read, men's clothing is outpacing cameras, computers and beer in online sales, likely because the online menswear market isn't saturated. Which is what the womenswear market is facing: saturation of brands and trends. So this growth has created a huge opportunity, which started out as a creative statement and is now being capitalized on by businesses worldwide.

How long does it take you to get a trend presentation together? It depends on the type of forecast and how far ahead it is looking to the future. The farther ahead the forecast, the more it requires in-depth research. If it's a macro trend, it generally takes around two months to research and two weeks to create the presentation and write the final copy. If it's an emerging trend report, or a catwalk report, it can take one to two weeks. It's just a matter of assessing the lifespan of the trend. In both cases, I hunt for findings that I think are defining the future. And having done trends and fashion design for sixteen years now – it's easy to spot when something is new or is coming back.

Have you seen changes in the business in the past few years? The biggest change I've seen is the commercialization of trend forecasting and the multiplication of new trend agencies focused on close-to-season or retail trends and, in contrast to that, the growth of agencies specializing in lifestyle, consumer behaviour and mindsets and less on design direction. As such the subscription business has had to evolve and trend agencies are pushing for advisory and tailored trend analysis for companies.

The other big change has been in the homogenization of womenswear and the mix and matching of trends within one look or collection. There are more and more synergies between trends and this has impacted both short term and long-term trends. Finally, the next biggest change has been the rise of menswear as a key presence in the creative fashion landscape, with much innovation and risk taking coming from that category, whereas in the past womenswear was more a birthing place and cesspool for experimentation.

How do companies/designers use trend information? Style industry companies save time and acquire a global view on trends through trend intelligence and expert analysis. It also gives them additional confidence in their decision-making process. The wrong colour choice can cost a clothing or shoe company a great amount of money. Aside from the glitter and dream the fashion industry presents to the world, it is essentially a manufacturing business. And a great deal of work, time, finance is at stake – let alone the environmental impact fashion manufacturing has. Therefore, companies rely on the intelligence provided by trend agencies with experts around the world, or consultants with a successful track record, to help them navigate this complex and fast-changing industry.

Another way fashion companies use trend agencies is as a one-stop shop for inspiration, when their design teams are pressed for time and need as much visual inspiration as possible to deliver, sketch and design a collection fast.

On the sales side of trends and what impacts retail, buying and visual merchandising, trend agencies help buyers with consumer product analysis, information on best sellers, key drivers and sales data to guide commercial decisions. And on the consumer lifestyle side of trends, analysts provide key information on the way mindsets and therefore future markets are shifting, where

7.13

there is opportunity or decline, change in behaviours, demographic issues and shifting social paradigms. Those, in turn, influence consumer engagement and these insights are key as they highlight innovations and opportunities in design, retail, branding, marketing, culture and media communication.

How can a fashion student benefit from trend knowledge? Trend forecasting teaches students how to edit key messages and images into a concise and clear viewpoint. It's important to have a cunning and selective eye when sifting through hundreds of images and articles of information and be ruthless in your choices. They also learn the difference between a macro and micro trend, as timing in fashion is everything. Students also gain a better understanding of how images relate to each other. For this they need to delve into the historical and anthropological aspect of fashion. Trends coexist with branding and what needs to be perceived by the viewer or consumer, so there are synergies with creative direction and marketing, which is of particular interest to burgeoning fashion designers. Finally, students learn to put aside their personal taste preferences and look purely at the markets and how they are evolving. This is key because as a designer and forecaster, you have to be able to switch hats and aesthetics depending on your client's needs.

What are the biggest menswear trends of the moment? The trends I have been noticing relate to some of the macro trends outlined earlier. There is a resurgence of interest in the 1940s and retro military clothing from that era. Punk is also a source of inspiration, mixed with DIY aesthetics, showing at times a dystopian and rebellious view of the world, which is being reinterpreted into tailoring. Playfulness is key as well, with designers hacking, colour blocking, reconstructing and taping into theatrical ways of dressing. Finally, androgyny and gender play underpin all of the above trends mentioned, with men redefining their roles in society and the way they express their identity through fashion.

7.13
Geraldine Wharry's final process is to translate her findings into designs through prints, sketches and garment customizations as in her collection titled 'SERIES'.

CHAPTER SUMMARY

This chapter provided you with an outline for starting and rising in your career as a trend professional. Consider the many roles you might play as you enter this exciting field: analyst/forecaster, colour or material specialist, freelancer, trade show trend planner/presenter, writer for a trade publication or fashion magazine, retail, or entrepreneur.

Pay attention to the details of how you present yourself in your CV, cover letters, portfolio, and interview approach. Get additional help for the elements that are not your strongest, reaching out to mentors, faculty, and peers while you are still in school, so you can make your best impression as you enter and progress in the ever-changing terrain of trends.

HOMEWORK ASSIGNMENTS
1. Go though job postings in job market websites, on trend agency websites or on brand websites. Look for your dream job and be ready to discuss in class.
2. Make a business plan by using a digital spreadsheet program.
3. Write down job roles that would benefit from trend knowledge and explain why.

DISCUSSION ACTIVITIES AND PROJECTS
1. Search online job portals by keying in the word 'trend' and/or 'menswear trends'.
2. Write a CV and cover letter describing briefly your strengths and employability.
3. Practice an interview session with a fellow student, asking about their strengths and weaknesses.

KEY WORDS
cover letter
CV
freelancer
portfolio

CONCLUSION

In this book, we have shown how to synthesize material from a vast pool of information and translate this into a presentable format that will allow you to inspire the audience you present it to and help them stay competitive. We began by demonstrating the importance of socioeconomic and cultural change to menswear consumer behaviour.

In the opening chapter of the book, 'Society, Menswear and Trends', we have explained which historical moments (wars, changes in leaderships, reactions to current economic climates) have influenced what men have worn. We included in this chronicle of trends the importance of *Fashion*, the London based menswear magazine, as well as the establishment of The Color Association of the United States (CAUS). They both affected how early trends were diffused throughout society: *Fashion* influenced the end consumers, and CAUS influenced the retailers.

In the second chapter, 'Defining Trend Thinking and Concepts', we defined concepts that are based on sociological theories from Everett Rodgers and Richard Dawkins, as well as popular thinkers such as Malcolm Gladwell. More importantly, we illustrated how to apply these theories to menswear. These essential theories will allow you to have a more systematic understanding of human behaviour.

In Chapter 3, 'Menswear Retail and Trends', the focus is on the retail (the largest and most important) end user of trend information. In this chapter we defined various types of retail and how each can benefit from trend analysis. We also defined menswear demography and psychographic characters that help to narrow down the target customer.

Chapter 4, 'Trend Details for Business', was dedicated to the business of trends. It showed an in-depth analysis of the catwalk, street style, and the trade show environment, and it explained how to cover the numerous aspects of fashion. We reviewed all three elements that influence the relationship between the retail and trend businesses by breaking them down into more workable segments.

Chapter 5, 'How to Research Trends', is central to the book, exploring what information to gather and where to look for it. The chapter explained which specific areas of the sociocultural landscape to consider when researching trends.

In Chapter 6, 'Application of Trend Data', we explored how to apply the trend information gathered – in other words, how to report your trends to an audience. We have provided step-by-step instructions as a guideline for putting together an effective presentation or a trend workshop.

Finally, in Chapter 7, 'Trends and the Industry', we outlined how to deal with the post-graduation world and how trend information can help you start or advance your career. We explained the essentials of CV writing and offered tips on how to survive the job interview. We also surveyed various professional roles, from working as a freelancer to owning your own agency.

Each chapter yields industry insight from the world's leading trend agencies, as well as experts explaining their methodology and their future projections. Reading them will inspire you to incorporate trend thinking into your educational curriculum and into your professional life. This perspective prepares you to progress in the competitive menswear market and, ultimately, to excel in your career.

REFERENCES

Albers, J. (1963/2006), *Interaction of Color*. New Haven, CT: Yale University Press.

Andersen, P. B. (2012), 'Where Is the Original Thinking', *Scenario* Magazine, 1: 10–11.

A. T. Kearney and The Consumer Goods Forum (2013), 'Understanding the Needs and Consequences of the Ageing Consumer'. Available online: http://www .theconsumergoodsforum.com/files /Publications/ageing_consumer_report.pdf (accessed 25 Feb 2017).

d'Aurevilly, J. B. (1897), *Of Dandyism and of George Brummell*. London: J. M. Dent. Available online: https://archive.org/details /ofdandyismofgeor00barb (accessed 16 Feb 2017).

Birren, F. (1945), *Selling with Color*. New York: McGraw-Hill. Available online: https://archive .org/details/sellingwithcolor00birrrich (accessed 25 Feb 2017).

Business Wire (2015), 'Menswear Will Contribute US$40 Billion Sales in the Global Apparel Market by 2019', March 30. Available online: http://www.businesswire.com/news /home/20150330005113/en/Menswear -Contribute-US40-Billion-Sales-Global -Apparel (accessed 25 Feb 2017).

Dawkins, R. (1976/2006), *The Selfish Gene*. Oxford, UK: Oxford University Press.

Delineator (1937), April: 24.

Edelkoort, L. (2012), personal conversation, Italy.

Euromonitor Research (2015), 'Trends in the Men's Fashion Market', *Euromonitor International*, March 30. Available online: http://blog.euromonitor.com/2015/03 /trends-in-the-mens-fashion-market.html (accessed 13 Mar 2017).

Eves, J. H., B. L. York, C. Buch and M. Palmer (2017), 'Sewing Revolution: The Machine That Changed the World', Windham Textile & History Museum. Available online: http://www.millmuseum.org/history /captains-of-industry/sewing-revolution/ (accessed 16 Feb 2017).

'Furnishing Editorial' (1894), *The Clothier and Furnisher*, February (7): 75. Available online: https://books.google.com/books/reader ?id=pisAAAAMAAJ&printsec=frontcover &output=reader&pg=GBS.PA32 (accessed 13 Mar 2017).

Geoghegan, J. (2017), 'Menswear growth to outstrip womenswear by 2020'. *Drapers*, January 9. Available online: https://www .drapersonline.com/news/menswear-growth -to-outstrip-womenswear-by-2020/7017443 .article (accessed 13 Mar 2017).

Gladwell, M. (2000), *The Tipping Point: How Little Things Can Make a Big Difference*. Boston, MA: Back Bay Books.

Grodzins, M. (1957), 'Metropolitan Segregation'. *Scientific American*, October. Available online: https://www.scientificamerican.com/article /50-years-ago-in-scientific-american-white -flight-1/ (accessed 22 Feb 2017).

'Growth of Menswear Market Outpaces Womenswear' (2016), *Mintel*, June 10. Available online: http://www.mintel.com /press-centre/retail-press-centre/mintels -15-menswear-fashion-facts (accessed 13 Mar 2017).

Jarman, D. (2010), *Chroma*. USA: University of Minnesota Press.

Keeps, D. A. (2015), 'We've Certainly Been "Mad" for Modern', *LA Times*, 16 May. Available online: http://www.latimes.com/home /la-hm-mad-men-20150516-story.html (accessed 25 Feb 2017).

'Maytime House Parties' (1933), *Apparel Arts*, III (I): 76.

Miller, A. (2007), *Dressed to Kill: British Naval Uniform, Masculinity and Contemporary Fashions, 1748–1857*. Greenwich, UK: National Maritime Museum.

Rogers, E. M. (2003), *Diffusion of Innovations*. Fifth edition. Free Press.

Shannon, B. (2006), *The Cut of His Coat: Men, Dress, and Consumer Culture in Britain, 1860–1914*. Athens, OH: Ohio University Press.

Simmel, G. (1904), 'Fashion', *International Quarterley*, 10: 130–155. Available online: http://www.modetheorie.de/fileadmin /Texte/s/Simmel-Fashion_1904.pdf (accessed 24 Feb 2017).

Simpson, M. (2002), 'Meet the Metrosexual', Salon.com, 22 July. Available online: http://www.salon.com/2002/07/22 /metrosexual/ (accessed 22 Feb 2017).

'trend' (2010), *Online Etymology Dictionary*. Douglas Harper, Historian. Available online: http://www.dictionary.com/browse/trend?s=t (accessed 16 Feb 2017).

'trend' (2017), *Merriam-Webster Dictionary*. Available online: https://www.merriam -webster.com/dictionary/trend (accessed 26 Feb 2017).

RECOMMENDED READING

Albers, John: *Interaction of Color: Revised and Expanded Edition*, 2006, Yale University Press.
One of the most influential books on colour that has stood the test of time since its original publication in 1963. The book focuses exactly as the title says on the interaction of colour, and how colour can change dramatically depending on its proximity or size of surface.

Barrett, Joanne: *Designing Your Fashion Portfolio. From Concept to Presentation*, 2012, Fairchild Books.
This book, geared towards the fashion graduate, has clear instructions on how to design an essential portfolio. The book also helps the student to evaluate his or her skills to have the best possible platform to market the work to the right target.

Bickie, Marianne: *Fashion Marketing. Theory, Principles & Practice*, 2010, Bloomsbury.
This is a good book on the basics of fashion business and marketing.

English, Bonnie: *A Cultural History of Fashion in the Twentieth Century: From the Catwalk to the Sidewalk*, 2007, Bloomsbury Academic.
This book compares societal events that acted as cultural catalysts to drive fashion ideas forward.

Feisner Anderson, Edith and Reed, Ronald: *Color Studies*, 2014, Bloomsbury.
A comprehensive book that covers the concept of colour from physiological to psychological effects. The book also discusses digitalization of colour and colour management systems such as Pantone. Clearly explained and illustrated book that give a solid foundation in the world of colour.

Flynn, Judy: *Research Methods for the Fashion Industry*, 2009, Fairchild Books.
Manual explaining in detail and in depth what academic research in fashion is. This is essential reading for understanding how to conduct and prepare a solid research path.

Holtzschue, Linda: *Understanding Colour, An Introduction to Designers*, 2011, Wiley.
This book provides a good overview on various aspects of colour and colour theory. It will also help you with composing the colour stories based on foundation colour information.

Jarman, Derek: *Chroma, A Book of Colour*, 2010, University of Minnesota Press.
A highly personal and moving story of colour that is part theory and part personal observation. The main reason to read this book over others is the verbalization of colour.

Knox, Kristin: *Culture to Catwalk. How World Cultures Influence Fashion*, 2012, Bloomsbury.
This book connects culture, fashion and catwalks to bring a better understanding to the complexities of fashion design and its presentation.

Koumbis, Dimitri: *Fashion Retailing. From Managing to Merchandizing*, 2014, Bloomsbury.
Concise book on the full retail model, from on-site to off-site venues, giving the reader a good overall understanding of how retail works.

Leach, Robert: *The Fashion Resource Book. Men*, 2014, Thames and Hudson.
A book that defines not only the items in the menswear wardrobe but also explains the histories how some of the items came to be.

Lindstrom, Martin: *Buyology: Truth and Lies About Why We Buy*, 2010, Crown Business.
A popular must-read for anyone interested in branding and marketing. Based on multimillion-dollar neuro-marketing research.

Martin, Raymond: *The Trend Forecaster's Handbook*, 2010, Laurence King Publishing.
An essential read for anyone interested in forecasting, this is an in-depth explanation of the research processes connecting to design development and product.

Mears, Patricia: *Ivy Style: Radical Conformist*, 2012, Yale University Press.
This book focuses on menswear from the early twentieth century to today. It demonstrates the importance of campus youth culture in the evolution of menswear.

Paulins, Ann and Hillery, Julie: *Guide to Fashion Career Planning. Job Search, Résumés and Strategies for Success*, 2016, Fairchild Books.
In-depth overview and guide on how to plan your career after graduation. The book has CV writing tips and general information on how to develop yourself as a brand ready for the marketplace.

Seivewright, Simon: *Research and Design*, 2012, Fairchild Books.
Good basic book on how to conduct creative research and how to translate the information into collections. The book gives a good view on how most fashion designers work.

Shannon, Brent: *The Cut of His Coat: Men, Dress, and Consumer Culture in Britain, 1860–1914*, 2006, Ohio University Press.
Although the book focuses on the menswear consumer culture of Britain, it is essential reading for anyone interested in the interaction between society and men's dress.

Udale, Jenny: *Textiles and Fashion*, 2014, AVA Publishing.
Introductory book on various aspects of textiles design and fibre production, including dyeing and various surface treatments.

Vinken, Barbara: *Fashion Zeitgeist: Trends and Cycles in the Fashion System*, 2005, Bloomsbury Academic.
Essential read to see how gender, sexuality, commerce and dandyism shaped and continue to shape the fashion system.

Yurchisin, Kim and Johnson, K. P.: *Fashion and the Consumer*, 2010, Bloomsbury.
This book chronicles the relationship between fashion and consumption, explaining the various levels of consumption done by the population.

INDEX

PICTURE CREDITS

Cover Photograph Ruggero Mengoni
Cover model Stefan Fugger

0.1 Getty Images Entertainment, Photo by Vittorio Zunino Celotto/Getty Images

Chapter 1

1.1 Edward Loevy, Getty Images
1.2 Public domain, via Wikimedia Commons
1.3 Getty Images Entertainment, Photo by Pietro D'Aprano/Getty Images
1.4 Archive Photos, Photo by Express/Express/Getty Images
1.5 Hyacinthe Rigaud [Public domain], via Wikimedia Commons
1.6 Hulton Archive, Photo by Hulton Archive/Getty Images
1.7 Archive Photos, Photo by Stock Montage/Getty Images
1.8 Archive Photos, Photo by Fotosearch/Getty Images
1.9 Mary Evans Picture Library
1.10 SSPL, Photo by Florilegius/SSPL/Getty Images
1.11–1.12 Anja Kirberg
1.13 Mary Evans Picture Library
1.14 Photo by Alex Dellow/Picture Post/Getty Images
1.15 Gamma-Rapho, Photo by Victor VIRGILE/Gamma-Rapho via Getty Images
1.16 Trendstop
1.17 Aki Choklat
1.18–1.21 Copyright © WGSN Limited [2015]
1.22 Photo by Claudio di Lucia
1.23 Aki Choklat
1.24 Frans Hals (1582/1583–1666) [Public domain], via Wikimedia Commons

Chapter 2

2.1 Blend Images, John Lund/Getty Images
2.2 Getty Images Entertainment, Photo by Kay-Paris Fernandes/Getty Images
2.3 Images left to right: Kenzo, Julian Zigerli, Y-3, Lanvin, all courtesy of Trendstop
2.4–2.8 Aki Choklat
2.9 Universal Images Group, Photo by View Pictures/UIG via Getty Images
2.10 Fashion Snoops
2.11–2.13 Aki Choklat
2.14 Getty Images Entertainment, Photo by Kay-Paris Fernandes/Getty Images
2.15 Gamma-Rapho, Photo by Victor VIRGILE/Gamma-Rapho via Getty Images
2.16–2.17 Aki Choklat
2.18–2.19 Gemma Barbetti
2.20 Aki Choklat
2.21 Ruggero Mengoni/Gemma Barbetti
2.22–2.23 Aki Choklat

2.24 Getty Images Entertainment, Photo by Frazer Harrison/Getty Images for Coachella
2.25–2.26 Christian Trippe
2.27–2.28 Trendstop
2.29 Images left to right: Kenzo courtesy of Trendstop, Mai-Gidah and Courtney Campbell
2.30 Images left to right: Maison Margiela, Bobby Abley, Gucci, all courtesy of Trendstop
2.31 Images left to right: Raf Simons, Les Hommes, all courtesy of Trendstop
2.32 Images left to right: Reggiani Ceramica, Wooyoungmi courtesy of Trendstop

Chapter 3

3.1 GC Images, Photo by FG/Bauer-Griffin/GC Images
3.2 Bloomberg, Waldo Swiegers/Bloomberg via Getty Images
3.3 Fashion Window, Photo by Heather Berrisford/Getty Images
3.4 Diverso London
3.5 Getty Images News, Photo by Jack Taylor/Getty Images
3.6 Universal Images Group, Photo by View Pictures/UIG via Getty Images
3.7 Moment Mobile, Alex Segre /Getty Images
3.8 Getty Images Entertainment, Photo by Rachel Murray/Getty Images for LACMA Costume Council
3.9 Getty Images Entertainment, Photo by Tristan Fewings/Getty Images
3.10 Getty Images Entertainment, Photo by Dimitrios Kambouris/Getty Images for IMG
3.11 DigitalVision, Plume Creative/Getty Images
3.12 Fashion Window, Photo by Ben A. Pruchnie/Getty Images
3.13 Fashion Window, Photo by Kay-Paris Fernandes/Getty Images
3.14 Getty Images News, Photo by Joe Raedle/Getty Images
3.15 Bloomberg, Chris Ratcliffe/Bloomberg via Getty Images
3.16 Getty Images Entertainment, Photo by Andrew H. Walker/Getty Images
3.17–3.20 Fashion Snoops
3.21 Joshua Vander Klipp
3.22–3.23 Ember Todd

Chapter 4

4.1 Getty Images Entertainment, Photo by Vittorio Zunino Celotto/Getty Images
4.2 Aki Choklat
4.3 Getty Images Entertainment, Photo by Kay-Paris Fernandes/Getty Images
4.4 Getty Images Entertainment, Photo by Ben A. Pruchnie/Stringer/Getty Images
4.5 Gamma-Rapho, Photo by Victor VIRGILE/Gamma-Rapho via Getty Images

4.6 Gamma-Rapho, Photo by Victor VIRGILE/Gamma-Rapho via Getty Images
4.7 Images left to right: Canali, Raf Simons, Marcelo Burlon, Canali, all courtesy of Trendstop
4.8 Corneliani, Valentino, N21, Fendi, all courtesy of Trendstop
4.9 Ruggero Mengoni
4.10 Gamma-Rapho, Photo by Victor VIRGILE/Gamma-Rapho via Getty Images
4.11 AFP, FRANCOIS GUILLOT/AFP/Getty Images
4.12 WireImage, Photo by Estrop/WireImage
4.13–4.15 Gamma-Rapho, Photo by Victor VIRGILE/Gamma-Rapho via Getty Images
4.16 Images left to right: Givenchy, Berluti, all courtesy of Trendstop
4.17 Getty Images Entertainment, Photo by Pietro D'Aprano/Stringer/Getty Images
4.18–4.19 Aki Choklat
4.20 Getty Images Entertainment, Photo by Kirstin Sinclair/Getty Images
4.21–4.22 Aki Choklat
4.23–4.27 Gemma Barbetti
4.28 Lucas Vasilko ©
4.29 Getty Images Entertainment, Photo by Ian Gavan/Getty Images for Graduate Fashion Week sponsored by George at Asda
4.30–4.32 BDA London

Chapter 5

5.1 Gemma Barbetti
5.2 Getty Images News, Photo by Spencer Platt/Getty Images
5.3 Surrey Nanosystems Ltd
5.4 Aki Choklat
5.5 WireImage, Photo by Julien Hekimian/WireImage
5.6 Getty Images Entertainment, Photo by Harold Cunningham/Getty Images
5.7 Getty Images Entertainment, Photo by Awakening/Stringer/Getty Images
5.8 By FaceMePLS from The Hague, The Netherlands (ArtZuid 2013) [CC BY 2.0 (https://commons.wikimedia.org/wiki/File:ArtZuid_2013_-_Erwin_Wurm,_Big_Pumpkin,_2009_(8988213472).jpg)], via Wikimedia Commons
5.9 AFP, FRANCOIS GUILLOT/AFP/Getty Images
5.10 Archive Photos, Photo by Robert Alexander/Getty Images
5.11 Getty Images News, Photo by Oli Scarff/Getty Images
5.12 Getty Images Entertainment, Photo by Elena Braghieri/Getty Images
5.13 Redferns, Photo by Gijsbert Hanekroot/Redferns/Getty Images
5.14 Getty Images Entertainment, Photo by Todd Williamson/Getty Images for AMC
5.15 Getty Images Entertainment, Photo by Stefania D'Alessandro/Getty Images

5.15 AFP, FRANCOIS GUILLOT/AFP/Getty Images

5.16 AFP, GIUSEPPE CACACE/AFP/Getty Images

5.17 Fashion Window, Photo by Kay-Paris Fernandes/Getty Images

5.18 Aki Choklat

5.19 Fashion Snoops

5.20–5.22 Aki Choklat

5.23 AFP, TIMOTHY A. CLARY/AFP/Getty Images

5.24 Aki Choklat

5.25 Modem Online (http://www.modemonline. com/fashion/)

5.26 Gemma Barbetti

5.27 Aki Choklat

5.28 Gemma Barbetti

5.29 MUNICH FABRIC START

5.30–5.32 Arvenco/Peter Betsche

Chapter 6

6.1 Gemma Barbetti and Photos of models by Estrop/WireImage/Getty Images

6.2 Concept & design: Sandy MacLennan; Illustration: Gary Kaye; Photography: Aaron Tilley; Courtesy of *Textile View* Magazine

6.3 Neva Turunen

6.4 Bloomberg, Photographer: Woohae Cho/ Bloomberg via Getty Images

6.5 Concept: Sandy MacLennan; Courtesy of John Smedley Ltd

6.6 Concept & design: Sandy MacLennan; Illustration: Gary Kaye; Photography: Aaron Tilley; Courtesy of *Textile View* Magazine

6.7 Aki Choklat

6.8 Gemma Barbetti

6.9 Aki Choklat

6.10 Images left to right: Salvatore Ferragamo, Marni, all courtesy of Trendstop

6.11 Aki Choklat

6.12 Getty Images Entertainment, Photo by David M. Benett/Dave Benett/Getty Images

6.13 –6.14 Aki Choklat

6.15 Neva Turunen

6.16 Aki Choklat

6.17–6.20 Gemma Barbetti

6.21 Aki Choklat

6.22 Trendstop

6.23 Claudio Scalas

6.24 Concept & design: Sandy MacLennan; Photography: Aaron Tilley & Sandy MacLennan; Courtesy of Pantone View Colour Planner

6.25 Concept & design: Sandy MacLennan; Photography: Aaron Tilley & Sandy MacLennan; Courtesy of Pantone View Colour Planner

6.26 Concept & design: Sandy MacLennan; Photography: Aaron Tilley & Sandy MacLennan; Courtesy of Pantone View Colour Planner

6.27 Concept & design: Sandy MacLennan; Illustration: Gary Kaye; Photography: Aaron Tilley; Courtesy of *Textile View* Magazine

6.28 Concept & design: Sandy MacLennan; Illustration: Gary Kaye; Photography: Aaron Tilley; Courtesy of *Textile View* Magazine

6.29 Concept & design: Sandy MacLennan; Illustration: Gary Kaye; Photography: Aaron Tilley; Courtesy of *Textile View* Magazine

6.30 Concept & design: Sandy MacLennan; Photography: Aaron Tilley & Sandy MacLennan; Courtesy of Pantone View Colour Planner

Chapter 7

7.1–7.2 Fashion Snoops

7.3 Aki Choklat

7.4 Concept & design: Sandy MacLennan; Illustration: Gary Kaye; Photography: Aaron Tilley; Courtesy of *Textile View* Magazine

7.5 Getty Images Entertainment, Photo by Ilya S. Savenok/Getty Images

7.6–7.10 Aki Choklat

7.11–7.13 Photography and Artwork by Geraldine Wharry

All reasonable attempts have been made to trace, clear and credit the copyright holder of the images reproduced in this book. However, if any credits have been inadvertently omitted, the publisher will endeavour to incorporate amendments in future editions.

ACKNOWLEDGEMENTS

I would like to thank all the colleagues, friends and family who helped me with the internationally complex, and yet rewarding research, especially Gemma Barbetti for her tireless work and commitment and Geordie Diaz for proofreading the manuscript.

The book is dedicated to all fashion professionals who work in and love the world of menswear.